Who Should Run the Health Service?
realignment and reconstruction

Olusola Oni

Consultant Orthopaedic Surgeon, The Glenfield Hospital, Leicester
Surgical Tutor, Royal College of Surgeons of England
Examiner, Royal College of Surgeons of Edinburgh
County Chairman, Hospital Consultants and Specialists Association

Radcliffe Medical Press
Oxford and New York

© 1997 Olusola Oni

Radcliffe Medical Press Ltd
18 Marcham Road, Abingdon, Oxon OX14 1AA, UK

Radcliffe Medical Press, Inc.
141 Fifth Avenue, New York, NY 10010, USA

British Library Cataloguing in Publication Data

A catalogue record for this book is available from the British Library.

ISBN 1 85775 169 8

Library of Congress Cataloging-in-Publication Data

Oni, Olusola O. A.
    Who Should Run the Health Service?: realignment and
  reconstruction/Olusola O. A. Oni.
        p. cm.
    Includes bibliographical references and index.
    ISBN 1–85775–169–8
    1. National Health Service (Great Britain)–Administration.
  2. Medical Policy–Great Britain–Decision making. I. Title.
RA412.5.G7055 1997
362. 1´0941–dc20   96–33577
CIP

Typeset by Advance Typesetting Ltd, Oxon
Printed and bound by Biddles Ltd, Guildford and King's Lynn

Dedicated to fellow harassed health professionals
grimly hanging in there.

Contents

Prologue

Doctors have genuine reasons to be hostile and/or apathetic to the idea of getting involved in hospital management. For a start, a significant managerial role involves a great deal of paper work – reading and writing – which may reduce clinical work and lead to a loss of skill; it may even interfere with private practice. Secondly, management is invariably poorly focused and is often not immediately relevant to clinical practice. Thirdly, committees are usually badly organized with committee meetings frequently involving protracted discussion on matters that may be essentially for information only; most meetings are held simply out of habit.

Once medical superintendents organized and ran municipal hospitals with the aid of a matron and a hospital secretary. The reorganization of the national health service (NHS) in the 1970s transferred decision-making about resources and management from hospitals to districts, to which doctors had little real access. At the same time, with the new structure, the power relationships between the three dominant NHS professions – medical, nursing and administration – altered, perhaps as intended. There was also for the first time restriction in NHS funding. The result of all these factors was to make it difficult for doctors to have an effective role. Even though Griffiths wanted to reverse this trend, the government chose to confine clinicians to a peripheral role in the new reforms.

Previously, medicine, like other great professions, was accustomed to managing its business. Today, most consultants direct and manage a private practice and general practitioners (GPs) are independent contractors to the NHS. As a result of the new reforms, however, the non-clinical staff have come to dominate NHS management totally. Purchasers determine what services are to be provided and the Patient's Charter has defined the parameters of practice. Various structures set up ostensibly to increase participation by clinicians in management are almost totally advisory. Most consultant groups are mere 'talking shops' for airing discontent. Successive governments have made it clear that they are open to ideas from managers but not from doctors.

In these circumstances, there are two options: consultants can opt out of the NHS altogether or they can get directly involved in management. For most consultants, for moral and/or ideological reasons, the first is probably not an option. Most consultants will keep faith with the NHS if it can be demonstrated that the problems are soluble. Many consultants will become managers if it can be shown that they alone are capable of managing the NHS efficiently and cost-effectively; and for several reasons they are. Firstly, they have a unique knowledge and influence over patient care. Secondly, their decisions about individual treatment ultimately determine the use of resources. Thirdly, they are the only 'permanent' staff of the NHS; whereas the average managerial career spans five years, that of the doctor spans some 40 years. Fourthly, as doctors have freedom over their work, they are likely to be freer than others in expressing contrary points of view. Fifthly, doctors are best placed to enhance the profile of the less 'glamorous' aspects of hospital business, such as medical records and X-ray films storage, that in fact determine clinical effectiveness. Sixthly, only doctors working with individual patients can determine individual priorities and choice. Finally, involvement in day-to-day clinical activity provides the doctor with the necessary knowledge and experience to inform the management process.

The framework

The objective of the NHS is to make services available to meet all individual health needs, whether in hospital, at the GP surgery or in the patients' homes. It is not responsible for *environmental health*, which is concerned with sanitation and hygiene, nor is it responsible for *occupational health*, which is concerned with the individual's place of work. In most respects, the NHS has been a resounding success. The criticisms levelled against it are actually not very serious ones, nor are they unique to it. Health services elsewhere in the world face similar problems which they, like the NHS, have not yet resolved. The real problem of the NHS is the constant, perpetual search for the 'right' method of management.

Success in the NHS depends primarily upon the professionals who provide the care. Therefore, it stands to reason that they should be involved in determining priorities for the distribution of resources and in ensuring that the limited resources are used as effectively as possible. However, this is not what happens in practice. The policy in the 1990s is to limit professionals to providing advice. Accordingly, in the new NHS, no one group of non-managerial workers predominates; doctors are rated no higher than nurses or other groups, including the non-clinical staff. All groups offer advice independent of one another and it is left to managers to 'compute' the different advice to make decisions. In theory, this task is informed by a number of factors.

Organizational

Man as an individual has biological and physical limitations and, there-fore, he seeks co-operation with others. As a consequence, he estab-lishes 'co-operative systems' or organizations in which he can interact with his fellow men. A *formal* organization is a 'co-operative' in which these interactions are co-ordinated and designed for a common purpose. Formal organizations succeed only because individuals communicate with one another and are willing to contribute to joint action. In every formal organization, the members do different things, ie specialize. They are provided with incentives which induce them to contribute to group action and there are 'rules' and a system of rational decision-making. The functions of the executive of such 'co-operatives' are to:

- maintain communication between members
- secure services from members for appropriate rewards
- facilitate and define the purpose(s) of the organization
- integrate the organization into one whole
- establish a balance between conflicting groups and events.

Thus, an organization may be defined as a group of 'like-minded members' created to achieve a particular purpose; a 'co-operative' established in the best interests of its members. More often than not, however, an organization is regarded as a process by which men, materials, machines and management are brought together to achieve efficient production of goods and services. Such organizations vary in complexity, hence, the tasks are grouped into a series of activities. The structure consists of positions and units between which there are relationships based upon responsibility, the exercise of power, accountability and upon the exchange of information. There are two basic processes in formal organizations; division of tasks and integration of tasks. Enterprises are usually organized according to one of three models: line, line-and-staff and matrix.

Line organizations

In a line organization, departments or units are based entirely upon primary activities. Primary activities are those activities that are essential for survival, profitability and growth. An organization needs to raise money to start and/or expand (ie finance); it needs to produce something to sell (ie production); its products need to be sold (ie marketing); and, in the long term, it needs to develop new products or improve existing ones (ie research and development). Therefore, line organizations are usually divided into these four units (Figure 1.1). Each unit consists of a few people under the supervision of a line manager or supervisor who answers directly to a managing director or chief executive. The advantages of a line organization include the

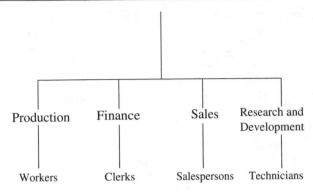

Figure 1.1: Line organization structure.

fact that the structure is easy to understand, responsibilities are well defined, individual contributions to the enterprise are readily discerned and there are few communication problems. The main disadvantage is that it becomes less effective as the organization grows in size. A 'compartment syndrome' sets in as people focus on the narrow content of the assigned functions.

Line-and-staff organizations

In a line-and-staff organization, there are two parallel vertical structures, line and staff (Figure 1.2). In addition to the line activities, staff

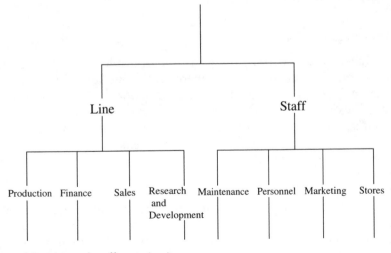

Figure 1.2: Line-and-staff organization structure.

or 'secondary' activities are performed by a cadre of 'specialists'. Staff activities are designed to 'improve' the efficiency with which line activities are carried out. An organization has to devote some time to industrial relations, to purchasing of raw materials and to quality control, etc. The staff function is of three varieties: advisory, service and control. In the advisory function, a nurse-manager may, for instance, be advised against a proposed course of action; a physiotherapist may be advised against the buying of a piece of equipment because of difficulty with maintenance; or a head of department may be advised on health and safety regulations. In the service function, the personnel department may provide a recruitment service for the whole hospital.

As in the line organization, each staff department consists of a few people under the supervision of staff managers who are also directly answerable to the chief executive. This organizational structure introduces greater complexity into interdepartmental and personal relationships and, as a result, there is often friction between line and staff personnel. A series of formal guidelines or principles may be needed to ease potential conflicts between line and staff. Staff functions are 'extracted' from existing chains of command (ie from the line arm of the organization), which curtails the authority of line managers. Line authority is diluted because staff activities are designed to produce greater economy and effectiveness of operations; the staff function is, after all, only there to introduce change in line. Staff managers tend to have a narrow outlook and are often not understanding of the problems of the 'shop-floor'.

Matrix organizations

In a matrix organization, there are two parallel vertical structures plus a third which derives its members from both line and staff (Figure 1.3). In practice, an additional horizontal structure is attached to a pre-existing, vertical organization. Line and staff personnel are temporarily loaned to a project officer. The notion of one person, one boss is given up in favour of multiple, but systematically shared, responsibilities. In its most common form, a 'task force' is superimposed upon the more traditional structures to adapt to the requirements of a particular piece of work bypassing the usual relationships.

The matrix structure is a highly effective means of focusing talent and resources on a specific goal, for example, undertaking a waiting list initiative or establishing a day ward service. The main advantages are firstly, that it breaks down the communication–authority barriers

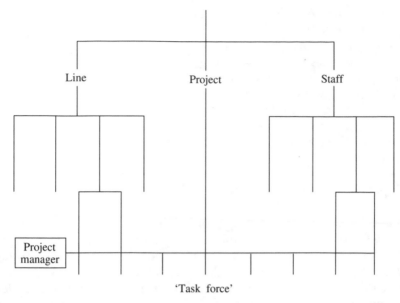

Figure 1.3: Matrix organization structure.

that exist in line-and-staff organizations and, secondly, that it provides an integrated approach to work. The disadvantages include complexity, which may result in inefficient use of resources, and its propensity to affect the career progress and development of individuals negatively, for there is no career ladder to climb in a matrix structure. Also, informal relationships become vital for success rather than formally prescribed ones. Finally, individuals are accountable to more than one boss, which can give rise to conflicting loyalties.

Large enterprises, such as the NHS, tend to be organized along the line-and-staff model. The job of co-ordinating the various activities of the enterprise is beyond the capabilities of one man, therefore, responsibility is delegated to subordinates, for example, directors or managers of departments. The pattern of command is militaristic. The usual procedure is for a staff manager to communicate with the 'shop-floor' through the line manager, since the staff manager has no direct line authority. Such relationships are called functional relationships; they are usually at the managerial level (ie above the heads of the frontline workers), and much of the communication in most large organizations is at this level.

A major problem with the NHS is that, although it is organized along the line-and-staff model, in reality it is a matrix organization.

The consultant 'firm' is akin to a 'task force'. The only difference between the two is in the permanence of the 'firm'. In its commonest form, the 'firm' consists of a consultant at its head, a lead nurse, usually the ward sister, who co-ordinates everything, and nurses and junior doctors. In some specialties, other paramedical staff, such as 'specialist' nurses, physiotherapists, speech therapists, occupational therapists, etc are included. In many ways, the 'firm' is also similar to a family; the consultant plays the 'father role' and the lead nurse, the 'mother role'. Putting aside the frequently trumpeted power conflicts, as a result of this arrangement patient care was 'co-ordinated' and the professionals worked as a team. In a well-run 'firm', the care plan for each patient was decided by one and all, at one or more weekly ward rounds.

Since the 1980s, this co-ordination of clinical work has been breaking down, however, and this cannot be good for patient care. In recent times, various members of the 'firm' have been encouraged, often unilaterally, to become 'independent'. Firstly, the nurses. They have rejected the traditional hierarchies of the 'firm'. Doctors are excluded from nursing matters and the ward sister no longer rules the roost. Clinical nurse specialists now determine nursing practice, producing protocols and guidelines often based upon inadequate data, and with little consultation. Nurses are enjoined to refuse to medicate if they disagree with the medical request. There is little medical input into day-to-day nursing, and vice versa; the ward round has given way to a casual, frequently unaccompanied, stroll around the ward by junior and senior doctors alike.

Thus, the previous 'care culture' is replaced by the 'production line principle' of every worker group for itself. There is no longer real communication between doctors and nurses. The 'named nurse concept' causes no end of trouble and frustration for doctors and relatives alike as they chase around looking for the 'right' nurse; even nurses on the ward complain about it. Nursing today is characterized by education way above what is required for the role and, as a consequence, nurses are rapidly and inexorably 'professionalizing' themselves out of the market. Many tasks previously performed by nurses have been ceded to the much cheaper 'auxiliaries'; very soon, with the appropriate vocational qualifications, they too will be allowed to medicate.

The matrix organization of medical work may sometimes produce an atmosphere of staleness or boredom since members end up performing the same tasks over and over again. This 'boredom factor' may be responsible for the agitation by nurses and their desire for 'job reprofiling'. No group is immune to it, however, for consultants also suffer from it in the form of 'burn-out'. The ward round as a 'debriefing session', where each member of a medical or consultant 'firm' could sound off and/or show off, was a very useful device. A periodic change of 'firm' activities, for instance, introducing a new line of treatment or procedure, or periodic reviews of care policy in which everyone takes part (ie not as isolated nursing or medical audit or initiative), could also relieve the 'boredom factor'.

Secondly, the junior doctors. As a consequence of the Calman initiative, a shorter working week and 'job reprofiling', their relationship with their seniors is no longer one of mutual dependence. Progressively, the camaraderie between senior and junior is being rent asunder. Hitherto, there has been an unwritten contract between junior and senior doctors – in return for 'free' training, the trainee looks after the consultant's patients. This contract is threatened and the consequences could be disastrous, for seniors may no longer feel obliged to train juniors free of charge. Several changes in hospital practice, such as day case surgery, pre-operative assessment clinics, specialist clinics and increasing use of non-medical staff as consultant assistants, have undermined the need for junior doctors in many areas. As a consequence, some trainees, particularly in the surgical specialties, now find that they have very little to do.

Economic

The market

In a 'free market', all goods and services are traded and exchanged freely by individuals. The quality and quantity of products are determined by the numbers who are willing to pay for them at a price automatically adjusted to 'equilibrium' (ie supply equals demand). By contrast, in a 'planned market', all economic activity is organized by a central authority – where to go and work, what to produce, how much to sell it at and to whom. Life is not as simple as this, however, for although frequently assumed to be the case, 'free markets' are not necessarily superior to 'planned markets'. Firstly, total freedom in the market-place will lead to anarchy; consequently, governments enact laws to prevent breaches of contract. Furthermore, in certain areas of activity, a free market could result in a morally unacceptable situation.

Secondly, the state often intervenes as it sees fit, although it acknowledges a central role for private enterprise in the provision of goods and services. This is the 'mixed economy' operated, for example, by the UK; here, the state:

- *supplements* the market – by providing services that the private sector will not supply, such as defence, police and prisons

- *restricts* the market – by providing services that the private sector can and does provide, such as health and education

- *distorts* the market – by taxation as well as by redistributing wealth

- *subsidizes* the market – by producing goods at below the true market price, such as roads and railways

- *controls* the market – by using public revenue and public expenditure to control the level of economic activities.

Thirdly, although in a 'free market' the number of goods may equal the number being demanded, not everyone is satisfied. Many people, for example, might desire a particular product but be unable to buy it for one reason or another. In particular, the 'free market' eliminates the poorest customers. Why should it always be the rich that get the goods? To satisfy everyone, government may set prices artificially low so that most people can afford the product. However, since there is a limit to what the economy can produce, demand will exceed supply and there will be shortages, for example, waiting lists. Although you never know when it will be your turn, this system is at least fair – allocation by lottery is certainly fairer than allocation by wealth. The main problem with this scenario is the lack of incentive to consumers, as well as to producers, and the challenge is to find methods of introducing incentives.

Where demand outstrips supply, attempts are usually made, often unsuccessfully, to increase the effectiveness in the market-place by:

- *repackaging* – 'understanding and responding' to the needs of the buyers cannot substitute for innovation

- *improving quality* – history abounds with companies that are first to develop or improve a product and yet have no market advantage (eg Apple Macintosh computers)

- *increasing production* – many products are available in large quantities and at low prices and yet they have not been able to find a market (eg coal)

- *hard sell* – success does not necessarily go to firms who sell the most efficiently

- *reducing costs* by closing facilities (ie 'downsizing') – usually shows rapid results in terms of financial performance but in the long term, it does not build for the future.

Planning

Economists believe that an extremely poor economy requires careful planning if it is ever to progress. The progressive decline of Third World economies is a testament to the bankruptcy of this approach. Rigid planning has also been suggested in situations, such as the NHS, where there are limited resources. However, the mechanism necessary for achieving this is itself very expensive and so part of the scarce resources are simply consumed by it. In this connection, it is estimated that NHS management currently consumes one billion pounds a year. It is no accident that the greatest achievements of man are often the works of mavericks and 'bumbling amateurs'. Economic planning, being usually informed by 'data', which are in the main mostly acquired in an unscientific manner, is totally blinkered to the foibles and unpredictability of human behaviour. In a study conducted by *The Economist* magazine in 1995, dustbin men (average hourly rate £4.70, and with little formal or continuing education) were found to be as accurate in economic forecasting as company chairmen (average salary £80 000) and well ahead of the finance ministers of the OECD.

The NHS is funded as part of public expenditure or expenditure financed from general taxation, national insurance and government borrowing. Public expenditure amounts to more than 50% of national income, hence, the government's desire to control it. This control is exercised via priority setting, efficient spending and spending as (parliament) intended. The government has to strike a balance between the necessity to intervene to remedy deficiencies in what the private sector provides and the fact that public expenditure may inhibit growth in private enterprise. Governments use various industrial policies, with varying degrees of success, to try and make the economy or a particular enterprise, such as the NHS, work better. They:

- encourage enterprise so that more people start up businesses

- promote improved efficiency through competition

- nationalize/privatize industries
- train the labour force to become more suited to industry's needs.

Finance

Finance is the main reason for introducing general management into the NHS. Hospital services receive three types of financial allocations, which are referred to as *revenue* (for day-to-day spending), *capital* (for new buildings, equipment, etc), and *earmarked* (for specific projects and collaborations). Each Trust owns its own assets – land, plant and equipment. In return, the Trust owes the government an equivalent amount called *original debt*. Part of this debt is given as interest-bearing debt (IBD) and part as public dividend capital (PDC). The Trust pays interest on the IBD and dividends on the PDC. To prevent a breach of the cash limits imposed by government, certain financial duties have been imposed on Trusts:

- obtain value for money
- break even – ie not show a deficit after paying costs of providing services, interests and dividends
- earn a predetermined return on assets
- live within predetermined borrowing (ie capital) limits.

Thus, the only financial freedom that the Trust has is freedom to plan expenditure. Compared with what previously obtained, therefore, NHS expenditure is very tightly controlled indeed, so much so that the potential for overspending is minimal. Contracts and pricing are carried out within specified rules. Prices charged to purchasers must cover costs, depreciation of assets, return on capital and other spending, such as insurance, remuneration for board members, etc. Financial performance is monitored periodically by the NHS Executive (NHSE), which is also involved in preparing business plans and strategic direction documents. Through the Capital Charging Scheme, there is now a comprehensive record of all fixed assets of the NHS and of all costs. In spite of all this, Trusts are still having great difficulty in balancing their books. Thus, although we are now able to count everything, the supply–demand mismatch continues. Therefore, the solution to the problems of the NHS lies elsewhere and not in financial management.

The financial difficulties that beset Trusts are caused primarily by underfunding, which is made worse by NHS inflation that is always significantly higher than general inflation. This is further compounded by the 'novel' financial rules, which are part of the 1991 reforms. According to these rules, NHS Trusts are obliged to make efficiency savings every year regardless of their financial situation. The effect of this is to require Trusts to treat more and more patients each succeeding year for less and less money which, of course, is impossible. The calculations of interests and dividends are based upon yearly appreciating assets. Since there is no real market for NHS assets, their valuation is arbitrary and a charade; this 'financial rule' merely serves to reduce the income of Trusts year on year as the 'mortgage' payment to government appreciates year by year. To satisfy these *Alice-in-Wonderland* 'rules', Trusts are having to transform into 'sweat shops', contract out services to charlatans and avoid the chronically sick. In spite of these 'rules', Trusts have been found to be more financially efficient than most hotel chains, high street stores and private hospitals.

Social

Work may be defined in terms of a 'market role' or activity directed towards the production of goods and services and which carries a value in exchange. Every enterprise has to solve the problem of getting its work done. The political system determines how this is achieved. *Coercion* may be used, for example as in slavery, to ensure that individuals perform their prescribed role. However, this presents a number of difficulties not least because it causes moral outrage and infringes individual rights. In any case, it is eventually counterproductive because slaves revolt or they develop the 'sambo personality' of servility and apathy. Instead, governments use the law of *property rights* (or the sanctity of private property), which invests power of control and use of things on owners, governments and shareholders. It frequently infringes on the principles of fairness and creates a 'them and us' situation, which causes workers to 'rebel' or form unions.

The political system also determines the ability of a worker to command goods and services. In this connection, governments make a distinction between those who sell their labour for a wage and those who derive their income from the ownership or control of the means of production. The owner is akin to a landlord and the worker to a tenant. The tenant has strictly limited rights – he/she cannot alter things and his/her tenancy is terminable at relatively short notice. By contrast, the owner enjoys almost limitless rights and security. In the market, the highest degree of control is achieved where a professional sells his/her skills directly to a customer for a fee; where a professional is paid a salary, his/her market situation is weakened. For the salaried, the nature of work has drastically changed in recent times. The mechanization of work has resulted in work in very large organizations, which introduces the problems of relationships. Specialization has resulted in the decline of craft skills and of the use of the 'intellect', in the loss of control over one's work and in alienation, dissociation and isolation. Bureaucratization has resulted in the emergence of a managerial ideology. The increased demand for professionals has resulted in conflict with managers who have a different value system, culture and outlook.

Work is the dominant influence in the life of most individuals. It takes up the major part of one's energies for most of the day, for most of the week, for most of the month, for most of the year, and for most of one's life. The occupation of a person provides a clue to his/her income, social standing, political outlook and interests. The kind of work that a person does profoundly affects the non-work areas of his/her life. Thus, if one is told that a person is a doctor or a nurse, one feels that one already knows a lot about that person. The social value of an occupation depends to some extent upon the position it occupies in the authority structure of an organization. The inferior status of the manual worker, regardless of his actual income, for instance, derives from his/her inferior position in the work-place. Status is also closely linked to 'political power'. In this respect, the NHS professionals have none of it. Doctors, for example, are in a state of *status ambiguous*; ie their status in the NHS is not entirely clear. On the one hand, it is clear that the NHS cannot exist without them, but on the other hand, they are treated as if they are the main problem of the NHS. At one time, they were accorded the lead role in the organization, but today, attempts are being made to undermine their authority.

In carrying out their roles, members of an organization are subjected to different, often conflicting, pressures. Although social or professional pressures, for example, may suggest that a doctor behaves in a certain way, the enterprise in which he/she works defines and spells out his/her activities. This lack of congruence causes strains between an individual and his/her organization and individuals adopt a variety of devices, such as informal organizations, collective bargaining, non-co-operation, etc to protect themselves.

2

The theoretical basis of management

The NHS has copied the management structures found in private enterprises, for services in the public sector have no tradition of this form of arrangement. Until the 1980s, hospital administrators were 'generalists', providing lay advice to the health professionals and lay administration for their hospitals. With the reforms, there has been a change from administrator (ie *mediator* of inputs and processes) to manager (ie *guarantor* of outputs and results).

Management has been practised throughout human history, but it is only recently that it has emerged as a separate academic discipline. Since the turn of the twentieth century, writers have put forward a number of theories on how to manage workers effectively and efficiently. These theories fall into three groups – classical, human relations and 'organic' – reflecting thinking and attitudes at a particular point in history.

The classical theory

The classical theorists sought to develop general principles that could be applied to all situations. The theory is based upon the desire to find the most economical way of increasing productivity by dividing tasks into their constituent parts. Much of this theory has endured and it has continued to provide the impetus for the study of management.

Scientific management

One strand, called scientific management, is mainly interested in industrial management and concentrates upon the 'shop-floor' and the behaviour of workers. It is concerned with formal structures and activities of the organization. It is based upon the belief that ignorance about the mechanics of tasks limits productivity and that workers often do not know how to do their job efficiently. Productivity is seen as the answer to both profit and wages. By analysing tasks and training workers in whatever new production methods arise out of this analysis, productivity could be increased (Figure 2.1). By linking work done to reward, it could motivate workers to do more.

Scientific management stresses four underlying principles for successful management:

- development of a true science of work

- scientific selection and training of workers

- bringing together the science of work and that of selection and training

- constant and interminable co-operation between managers and workers.

It is based upon systematic observations and measurement of tasks. The best technique of performing a task, for example, shovelling, is determined from a scientific analysis of that task and the worker is trained in that method. Work is separated into its different constituents and these are then distributed to 'specialists'. Scientific management underpins the 'closed-shop' or job-demarcation principle.

A major criticism of scientific management is that it is based upon a false image of man. The assumption on motivation is incomplete and is based almost entirely upon the economist's view of man. In practice, scientific management dehumanizes work and reduces it to boring repetitive tasks. Workers are demotivated because they are not trusted

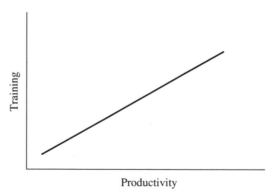

Figure 2.1: The training–productivity curve.

and are not allowed to identify with the employing company. There is little discretion for individual control over working methods. Managers, who are not personally involved, are encouraged to assume greater knowledge about the detail of a worker's duties than the worker himself and to assume that they are never wrong. Since one best way to do a job is rarely discernible and the fastest way of completing a job is not necessarily the most efficient, the effect of scientific management methods is totally unpredictable.

Scientific management does not provide a good working model for managers. It is concerned with design and organization of work for others rather than with design and functioning of executive work. It contends rather naively that there is only one best way of doing a job, which can only be derived from exact study and analysis. Thus, a major duty of the manager is to develop a science for each element of a man's work and to train him appropriately. This is an impossible task. Another criticism concerns the fact that the concept strengthens 'staff' function at the expense of 'line' or productive function.

Administrative management

A second strand, called administrative management, concentrates upon management's role throughout the organization and aims to identify principles of effective management that could be taught. It identifies elements of management function (Figure 2.2) as follows:

- *planning* – predicting the future and deciding today what needs to be done in the future. This elaborate way of looking at things suits the corporate bosses better than line management

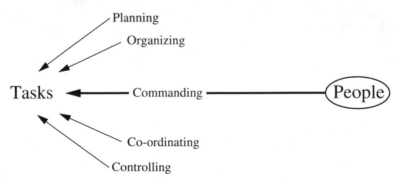

Figure 2.2: Getting things done through people.

- *organizing* – dividing work and allocating tasks to people and departments or teams

- *commanding* – issuing instructions to ensure that targets are met. This invokes a military parallel and a commander able to keep subordinates primed to undertake specified duties

- *co-ordinating* – uniting efforts. Disparate efforts have to be bound together effectively to give the customer what he/she wants

- *controlling* – setting targets, monitoring activity to ensure targets are met and taking remedial action as necessary.

Administrative management cites 14 principles for successful management, which include division of work, authority and responsibility, discipline, unity of command, unity of direction, remuneration, centralization, scalar (hierarchical) chain, order and stability of tenure.

A major criticism of administrative management is that managers are hired mainly to act the role of 'machines' and are used merely to achieve a particular end, say cost-cutting. On the other hand, full executive control is not possible because every worker's contribution to an enterprise involves the ability to use intelligence and intuition. Any attempt to achieve this will generate conflict.

Bureaucracy

A third strand of the classical theory, modelled upon the military's command structure and named *bureaucracy*, states that hierarchy, authority and bureaucracy lie at the heart of all formal organizations. It constructs an organization in the form of tiers of authority (Figure 2.3). The theory separates policy-making from operational control. Management relies on existing rules and precedents which relieve officials of the need to exercise discretion. The proponents of bureaucracy claim it to be the most rational and the most efficient form of administration; tasks are distributed rationally, duties are defined precisely and interactions are governed by rules.

Two elements of bureaucracy have been identified as follows:

1. hierarchy – stratification of officials linked in a continuous chain of command. Power and activity increase as one moves up the ladder. This is apparently essential to the controlling function, to ensuring proper behaviour and to providing adequate channels of communication

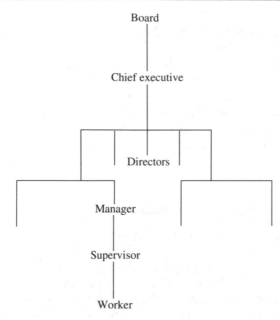

Board

Chief executive

Directors

Manager

Supervisor

Worker

Figure 2.3: A bureaucratic (hierarchical) structure.

2. division of labour – each official in the hierarchy is allotted specific tasks. This apparently increases expertise and makes training relatively quick and easy.

A major criticism of the bureaucracy model concerns its confusion of structure with function. According to this approach, it is not necessary to understand the business of an enterprise in order to run it; one becomes a leader and exercises authority not because of any personal attributes but merely because of one's position in the hierarchy. There are serious discrepancies between this model of rational organization and reality. It assumes administrative staff have professional expertise as well as the right to issue orders. Hindered by 'red tape', it is stifling of initiative and encourages unthinking conformity. The theory is concerned almost entirely with executive or 'staff' work. Those who are engaged in making the products of the organization are excluded and rated no higher than tools and machinery. Workers are regarded as the 'problem' of the organization and are excluded from participation in decision-making.

The human relations theory

This theory considers the people within an organization – their social needs, motivation and behaviour (Figure 2.4). The central message is that attitudes to workers may be more important to efficiency than physical or material factors, since individuals bring more to the workplace than their labour. People bring a range of psychosocial needs, which managers need to understand, since individuals are their prime assets. The *human relations* movement stresses two aspects of organizations:

1. matching machinery with methods
2. integrating these with the social system.

The theory was developed as a consequence of falling production and standards in the 1920s and 1930s. The Hawthorne experiments had revealed that workers are motivated in part by social factors and are capable through these means of determining and regulating productivity regardless of the organizational goals and targets. According to the human relations theory, group relationships are far more important in determining worker behaviour than physical conditions and/or working practices enforced by management. Wage levels are not the dominant motivating factor for most workers. Productivity is reduced by rigid division of labour and workers are more productive when given a wide range of tasks. Proponents stress leadership as being a key to effective management. The theory stresses that a manager is a leader and that understanding how leadership emerges is central to understanding management itself.

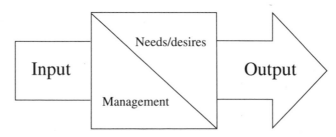

Figure 2.4: The human relations effect.

The human relations theory overestimates the desire of workers to participate in decision-making. It fails to recognize conflicts within groups within an organization and the influence of political and other social factors. It is simplistic and excessively altruistic. Technical performance is assumed, without any justification, to derive from work content.

The 'organic' theories

Research into the structures of organizations other than industrial concerns has led to the development of other theories.

Systems theory

This theory compares organizations with organisms. It emphasizes the complex nature of an organization with its different contributory variables. It seeks to explain and predict the behaviour of organizations by studying people, structures, process and environment. It believes that an organization is a collection of interacting parts that have to be viewed as a whole. Basically, an organization consists of subsystems which convert inputs of financial, human and material resources into outputs of goods and services, as follows:

- *psychosocial subsystem* – individuals and groups
- *technical subsystem* – the process of transformation, nature of input and output
- *information subsystem* – collection and analysis of data necessary for decision-making
- *managerial subsystem* – designs and administers the organization.

The 'organic' concept posits pragmatic, adaptive management – one situation may require an authoritative approach whereas another requires a relaxed, democratic manner. Thus, effective management quickly and accurately identifies key factors underlying a particular situation and responds to it. An *open system* (Figure 2.5a), such as a business concern that has an ill-defined boundary, needs to relate to suppliers and customers from whom it receives inputs. It needs to interact with its environment, that is, people, machinery and materials which it uses to make things. A *closed system* is self-supporting and is

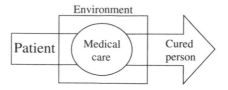

a) Open system

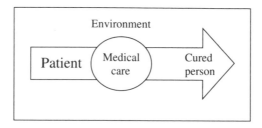

b) Closed system

Figure 2.5: The systems concept.

not dependent on the outside world for survival. It does not interact with the environment in which it exists (Figure 2.5b).

Central to this treatise is the belief that subsystems seek equilibrium when disturbed by internal and/or external forces; social values cause a system to seek the equilibrium state when so disturbed. According to this theory, it is the duty of the 'higher classes' to provide the leadership necessary for maintaining the system in the state of equilibrium. It has not yet been possible, however, to demonstrate interdependence between variables. The systems theory is an abstract concept, difficult to apply in practice. Relationships and environments are usually complex and impossible to analyse systemically. The theory is essentially descriptive, detailing how organizations hang together, but offers no explanation for motivation, etc.

Contingency theory

This theory states that management is dependent upon context or situation (Figure 2.6), ie management style, organizational structure and workings of an enterprise are determined by the environment in

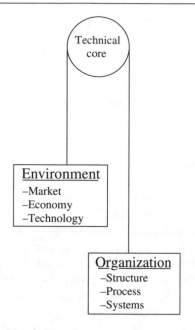

Figure 2.6: Situations calling for management.

which the organization exists. The ways in which a group should or may be organized are limited by a variety of practical and technical factors. For example, organizational structure depends upon size, nature of output, physical and intellectual nature of operations, relationship with 'markets' and relationship with other organizations. A large organization is able to decentralize many advisory and managerial tasks to specialists and to allow its top job-holders to rely on formal or written rules rather than personal supervision.

The theory asserts that an organization is a set of interrelated parts influenced by the wider society. A successful management is able to identify patterns for the functioning of systems in different environments. The principles are:

- *differentiation* – as systems become larger, they need to be broken down into smaller parts

- *integration* – to operate successfully, the functioning of the parts has to be integrated.

The contingency theory invents and exaggerates the importance of organizational goals at the expense of individuals. It has no consistent general principles and lacks predictability. There are several potential variables; therefore, it is impossible to distinguish key factors. Technology or working environment may, for example, make it impractical to use anything other than a particular approach.

Chaos (proactive management) theory

This theory developed in response to the fact that modern enterprises exhibit 'champ–chump' (ie 'boom–burst') cycles. This characteristic is apparently a result of the unpredictability of the organization's environment, including inputs, competitors, customers, technological revolution, etc. The command-and-control (ie *classical*) theories apparently provide no answer, because they encourage the formation of large organizations that are weighed down by inertia, expensive internal coordination and ineffective use of human resources. They also encourage specialization, which locks in place narrow job jurisdictions (ie the 'closed-shop' syndrome), which were previously painstakingly invented by managers, whereas workers today are being pilloried for adhering rigidly to them.

Success apparently depends upon the enterprise's ability to improve quality and service through innovation and constant improvement aimed at new markets (Figure 2.7). This necessitates that the 'shop-floor', the prime source of quality, be placed high in the organization's pecking order. Proponents have concocted as management theory, prescriptions for success derived from five ingredients: responsiveness

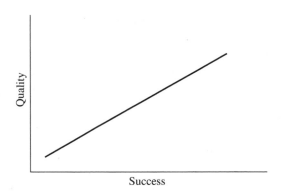

Figure 2.7: The quality–success curve.

to customers, constant innovation, wholesale participation by all connected with the organization, leadership that loves change and control by means of simple support systems. The theory proposes simple organizational structures, minimum bureaucracy and few management staff, proactive with 'hands-on' management and achievement-based promotion and great concern for customer welfare.

Another variation of the theory questions conventional management wisdom and emphasizes communication, direct personal involvement of management on the 'shop-floor' and teamwork. Data from role models apparently reveal certain elements of organizing an enterprise to achieve success:

- *people* – successful enterprises organize around people. People are motivated by being in control, belonging, being intellectually exercised and by being acknowledged for their achievements. Enterprises act for, and on behalf of, people; every act of a business has social consequences

- *profits* – putting profit first is not necessarily the best strategy for enhancing profitability

- *strategy* – anticipating and responding to customer needs – innovation, satisfaction, cost, etc.

3

Reflections on the 'management' thing

Management is predicated upon a belief that an enterprise can only run efficiently if there is central planning and control by a unit 'independent' of the frontline staff. In many instances, however, management appears to have materialized as a means of outfoxing the opposition, especially the workers. Consequently, it has been cast in a range of symbolic guises, from agent to quisling. The first managers were agents of owners; plausible fingermen who were likely to get away with whatever scam was being attempted. The status of managers changed with the increasing sizes of organizations in the nineteenth century. From then on, to be 'manager' no longer meant simply to be another type of worker but to be a 'non-worker'. The Americans began the process of stuffing it full of legitimacy and sympathetic academics began the task of isolating it from what other workers did. Thereafter, the reality of management moved from doing something to simply meaning something.

At one time or another, managers have provided a means of softening the distinction between masters and men (Figure 3.1), acting as a buffer between the binary extremes of society, a balm for soothing labour conflicts and rationalization for the relentless march towards wealth and dominance. The fantasy of conflict-free industrial relations has fooled everyone. The language – leadership, ownership, stakeholding, common purpose, teamwork, quality, communications, etc – has often persuaded professionals, supervisors and line managers to act as cushion between the top and bottom of what is often a very long hierarchical chain.

What does management really mean?

Management is defined by devotees as an endless cycle consisting of planning, implementation and control (Figure 3.2). Managerial tasks are perceived as organizing and supervising the work of others and

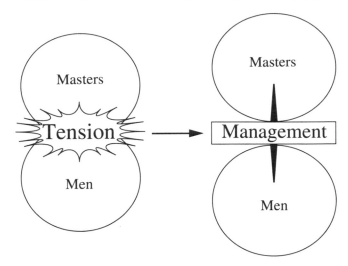

Figure 3.1: The master-and-men conflict.

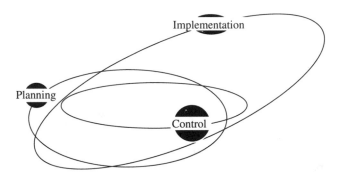

Figure 3.2: Management is an endless cycle.

supplying ideas and information. Management is regarded as the governing organ of an enterprise that is large and complex, in which a variety of tasks needs to be integrated and synchronized. Management is said to indicate function as well as the person discharging it and social position as well as authority. Apparently, without management, things will go out of control, there will be chaos, plans will fail to translate into action and the enterprise will flounder and stagnate.

In practical terms, general management is separated into three major functions:

1. *policy formulation* – carried out by a board or executive committee

2. *operational* or *line activities* – organizing what the enterprise was set up to do in the first place. Line activities comprise business generation (ie development of products or services, marketing and selling) and demand satisfaction (ie manufacture or delivery of service)

3. *support* or *staff activities* – ensure operational activities can take place (ie administration–planning, finance, personnel, etc).

Managers are charged with overseeing these functions.

However, things are not what they seem. The process of management is often far removed from customers (Figure 3.3) and from those who actually make the products. It is entirely peripheral to the central process of transforming input into products, of converting these to revenue and of using that to purchase new raw materials to begin the cycle again. Management is an idea that largely resists clarification. It is a nebulous concept similar to 'moral values'; that is, one about which people feel approving and which they wish to preserve in a good, idealized state and one that is so vague as to defy scrutiny in any

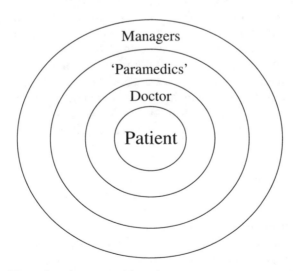

Figure 3.3: Hierarchy of contact with patients.

great detail and be difficult to knock. It is a concept about which a large number of highly paid, otherwise intelligent, people are willing to think, talk and write without ever ascertaining exactly what is meant by it.

Successful enterprises abound that do not have management at their helm. Universities, for example, manage well with administrators and the armed forces with commanding officers. German enterprises are run successfully without managers: they have 'managers' in the sense of people running things but no management movement or a specialized management language. Defined as a means of effective deployment and use of resources, 'managerial techniques' must have been deployed in moving huge masses of rock to construct the pyramids, yet the Egyptians had no professional managers. Specific 'managerial activity' cannot be distinguished from other activities that occur within employing units. For example, nurses have to deal effectively with resources and co-ordinate with others; doctors measure, analyse and plan ahead just like business executives.

The typical modern manager knows all the answers and he/she is encouraged to think so by the prevailing 'management doctrine'. Consequently, he/she plans, organizes and controls the work of others, ie the 'subordinates'. Employees are commodities to be managed but other managers, being self-motivated and interested in doing good work, are helped to develop and contribute. Co-workers in other departments, particularly the professionals, are enemies to fight. Those who are co-opted to participate in decision-making are used only as conduits for handing down edicts or as tools to 'salvage' mistakes. Managers have developed a number of 'feel good' devices to make this palatable.

Management, not being a true academic discipline, has no shared paradigm for generating new ideas, no agreement on existing facts and no clear guidance as to what makes a good or a bad manager. To fill the vacuum, modern management has resorted to what can only be described as the 'sound-bite' culture and a whole new lexicon has been developed. In this culture, packaging is regarded as more important than content. Many managers seem to believe that following half a dozen simple rules is the key to achieving goals. Others think that 45 minutes spent listening to a management guru is more important than knowledge, skill and hard work. The 'sound-bite' culture is damaging to the efficient running of the health service and, for several reasons, it is ultimately unworkable.

The management movement is full of contradictions. Most of the pioneers of formalized management were engineers but, when business schools were founded, they were designed for the needs of corporate bosses, who are mostly non-scientists. Successful management is akin to successful rat-catching; once the goal is achieved, there is nothing left to do. 'Modernization' of management by the 'revisionists' has had no effect whatever on cultural assumptions about conduct and power, and the new executive class has continued to behave in pretty much the same way as the old owners used to, ie in an autocratic manner.

Management has authority without direct line responsibility; it produces nothing yet seeks to dominate those who do. It takes no personal risks since failure can be blamed on someone else; workers, ie 'not doing enough', or owners, ie 'not investing enough'. Management, like cancer, once established is out of the control of the 'owners' of the enterprise and of its workforce. This is why the bosses of the privatized utilities could pay themselves huge salaries and bonuses as the government, shareholders and workers stood by helplessly. This is why a Yorkshire water company could offer a poor service and then have the temerity to blame its customers for its inadequacies. This is why the 'City of London', although not an elected body or one with any constitutional standing, could hold governments to ransom and determine the direction of economic policy.

Profession or science?

Management cannot be regarded as a profession because it does not fulfil the criteria of a profession. No formal education is necessary and there are no universally accepted set of rules governing its practice. It is not characterized by an established, systematic body of knowledge acquired over several years of intellectual training. There are no ethical standards and codes of practice laid down by a 'statutory' body. Entry is not restricted to those possessing predefined qualifications or experience. There is no brotherhood of managers united in ideals, purpose or *modus operandi*; and management has so far not been successful in training any top business executives.

Management as a specialism is a product of Anglo-Saxon culture. It did not develop through the process by which professions have traditionally emerged (Figure 3.4), ie identification of specialized activity, formation of a profession and, thereafter, establishment of standards for legitimization. Instead, management began life as a demand for legitimization, followed by the formation of the 'profession' and then began the hunt for specialized activity. Unlike true professions,

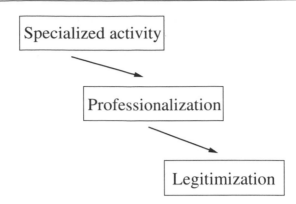

Figure 3.4: How professions have traditionally evolved.

the culture of management is obsessed with status rather than with action.

Management is not a science because it possesses no testable knowledge. There is no body of arcane knowledge that could distinguish management from other callings. Managers do not work in a predictable enough manner for their work to be treated as a science by unbiased observers. There are no techniques of management that could be used consistently and/or successfully in the normal course of 'managerial' work. Management theories are not able to predict organizational reality, so that a manager does not know with any certainty what to do to achieve an organization's goals effectively and efficiently.

To most people, management is neither interesting nor useful and, as a result, managers strive most strenuously to impress. They use words in the hope that no one will notice that they do not know what they are talking about. They try very hard to be like scientists but with little success. Since they are dealing with human nature which is unpredictable, they cannot conduct controlled experiments and are unable to establish the true nature of the relationship between one variable and another. Therefore, they are prone to change the evidence rather than alter a theory.

A management theorist (managerist) uses data to prove his/her theory rather than to examine it. Consequently, each and every management theory is valid and has a following. It is a lottery to decide which point of view to believe. By contrast, when a scientist comes upon a problem, he/she formulates a theory, then carries out a controlled experiment and obtains data to examine his/her theory. If the data are supportive, the theory becomes established and is disseminated for others to confirm or refute. If the data are not supportive, the theory is rejected, abandoned and expunged.

What do managers actually do?

We know what doctors do – diagnosing and instigating treatment; we know what nurses and other paramedical staff do – carrying out treatment and care plans; we know what administrators, the organization's 'midwives' do – ensuring bills are paid, contracts are honoured and plant and machinery are in good working order. By contrast, no one is quite sure what managers really do. The work appears to involve mostly 'clerkish' activities, that is, dealing primarily in the symbolic world of words and numbers. A manager is that person designated to enter into contracts on behalf of the enterprise, sign cheques and hire and fire other employees. He/she is not involved in details of the enterprise's activities but concentrates on the 'broad picture'.

In practice, the main task appears to be 'information gathering' and, hence, it is characterized by:

- *a lack of schedule* – constant interruptions, short contemplative periods (10–15 minutes)

- *not much desk work* – few written works, most time spent 'discussing'

- *fleeting contacts.*

These, the main activities of management, are dressed up in colourful metaphors by management writers. They suggest that the work of management is characterized by superficiality, that management is an intuitive and extemporizing activity, dealing commonsensically in the here-and-now. 'Managerial' work has been associated with speed, variety, brevity and discontinuity; with the exercise of power based upon informally acquired information; and with decision-making on the hoof, rarely in an orderly, logical, step-by-step manner, relying instead on flair and intuition.

What managers actually do is different from the popular conception, however, and managers themselves often harbour many illusions about the nature of their work. For example, managers emphasize making regular contacts with workers but diary enquiry reveals that this is done very infrequently. Up to 50 per cent of managerial time is spent away from the businesses, yet no arrangements are made for covering such absences. This raises the question as to whether managers are overvalued with regard to direct influence on the workings of the enterprise they manage. Less than 10 per cent of time is spent on any task requiring sustained attention, which suggests neglect of policy matters.

There is evidence to suggest that there is no requirement for management in the NHS on the scale that has happened since the 1991 reforms. Firstly, clinical work is knowledge based, so that most health workers know more than their managers. Knowledge-based work, as distinct from 'manual' work, cannot be designed for the worker but only by the worker him or herself. Often, management has no direct identification with the product and little contact with the customer. There is no possibility of regular feedback so that the degree to which management actually understands the business is limited. Secondly, there are rapid changes taking place in the NHS at the moment. Ideas need to be developed frequently and implemented simultaneously. This requires considerable input from the 'shop-floor'. The requirement for management in these circumstances is for facilitation and co-ordination rather than for control. Thirdly, the social trend since the 1960s has been towards personal freedom in all areas of life. Therefore, workers in general are less happy to be constrained than they were at the birth of the NHS.

The progressive, and relentless, nature of the commercial and economic decline of the UK over the last two or three decades is a testimony to the lack of success of management. Managerial power has been inversely related to economic power. This is not surprising. Management works only in an authoritarian culture and/or where there is an element of coercion in the political system. This *locus standi* is at the root of the economic miracle of mass production and of the 'tiger' economies of the 1990s. In the UK for some time now, there has been a lack of synergy between the politics of the work-place, with its deference to managerial control, etc, and the politics of society at large, with its unbridled freedom. In these circumstances, management has become an anachronism, being totally out of phase with societal dynamics. This lack of synergy is responsible for the failure of managers to halt the progressive decline in economic power. It is also responsible for the industrial battles of the 1980s which the workers, unfortunately, lost because of an intellectually limited leadership.

4

General management and the NHS

The negotiations which preceded the birth of the NHS sought to harmonize a medical profession split into very different groups with separate terms and conditions of employment. General practice was akin to a small business and each practitioner was, in the main, independent of the hospital service. Hospital doctors were more varied; while some worked for 'voluntary' hospitals in which they held enormous and independent power, others worked in 'municipal' hospitals ruled by local politicians through a senior doctor, the Medical Officer of Health. Therefore, in the new national health service, the general practitioners became independent contractors to the service, receiving a capitation fee for each patient on their list, whereas consultants became salaried within a 'voluntary' hospital model. Although the profession was now subordinate to the NHS, the freedom of each doctor to practise as he or she saw fit was not diminished; medical organization was syndicalist in nature.

The deed

For 40 years the NHS was managed with few administrative constraints. Central control was exercised only through fiscal measures by ministers and civil servants. The doctors provided leadership and were supported in this role by administrators. However, strictly speaking, there were no subordinates; doctors looked after themselves, the matron commanded her nurses and the administrator gave orders to his/her clerks. Private hospitals are still being run along these lines. In spite of this rather flimsy management structure, the NHS was, by all business standards, a huge success. Medical care was of the highest technical quality and was available to all at a very low cost, and the numbers of patients treated increased year-on-year.

In 1974, with the pretext of introducing coherent local planning within the framework of the NHS, the service was given a new corporate structure designed by management consultants. New layers of management were inserted and local institutions were clustered together. To create a role for the new management, elaborate planning systems were introduced and a new cadre of administrators metamorphosed. The method of management was still by consensus, as teamwork was thought to be the only structure suitable for the health care enterprise. It was felt that, since all health workers were professionals, no group of workers should have the upper hand. As a result of this reorganization, there was a significant shift of power from medical to non-medical staff, particularly nurses. Consensus management was plagued by the elaborate consultation required before any change could be effected, although, as a result, it minimized the number of 'white elephant' projects. Consensus management was blamed for all the problems of the NHS, which were, in reality, manifestations of the size and complexity of the organization.

By the late 1970s, management was being perceived as the 'new' profession. Politicians had run out of ideas as to what to do with the escalating costs of public services. The managers, with their 'scientific' training, were perceived as white knights who would come to the rescue. According to the thinking prevalent at the time, businesses and organizations had problems because they lacked proper management. Therefore, in 1981, one of the canards of management, annual performance reviews, was introduced into the NHS to monitor each tier of the service systematically. The Griffiths reorganization which followed installed a single leader or general manager to every tier. Whereas in the old system, administrators merely chaired meetings of management teams, in the new system, each general manager was a real boss. The manager, a 'generalist', and not the professionals now decided everything; the structure of the organization, the division of labour, the training required for each job and so on. The organization became more important than the service or 'product'. Consequently, the new management was deliberately anti-professional and the professions were effectively excluded from the board of directors. The essence of general management is that professional hierarchies are subsumed and thereby cease to exist altogether.

The consequences

The new NHS management has had deleterious effects on the NHS without delivering the cultural changes predicted for it. Consultants have become disenfranchised and disillusioned, the quality of the managers is poor, transactional costs have soared and there are now interminable confrontations between managers and professionals. Managerialization has not delivered the nirvana: the waiting list problem has not been solved; there is continued waste and inefficiency; the morale of health workers is low; and there are now more complaints about the service than ever before. To what extent has the new NHS management contributed to this state of affairs?

In the old NHS, there was an informal contract between professionals (Figure 4.1), ie between a patient's GP and his/her consultant, with regard to treatment and care. In this arrangement there was partnership and equality of status between consultants and GPs. In the new NHS, the contract is more formalized and it is specifically between GPs and managers. As a consequence, the consultant is no longer a partner in the care of his/her patients. At best, he/she has been transformed into a technician, at worst, a 'mechanism' for making money for the Trust. Trusts now appear to belong exclusively to managers, with the consultant, the ultimate provider and legal guardian of patients, treated as just another employee. This demeaning of the consultant status has denied their work any intrinsic interest. The result is low morale and the destruction of the bond between Trusts and their doctors. Little wonder then that in many specialties it is becoming more and more difficult to recruit consultants.

Figure 4.1: Medical care 'contract', then and now.

As part of the reforms, many managers were recruited from outside the NHS and, therefore, had no prior training in health matters. In addition, most also have very little understanding of finance, and decision-making is of low quality. The present chaotic state of the NHS and the requirement for an army of outside consultants reflects the lack of expertise of the new management. Bringing in managers from elsewhere to run the NHS is like asking a gynaecologist to fix a broken leg. In the short term, he will require the expertise of others (ie outside consultants) and in the long term, he will have to retrain (ie become an orthopaedic surgeon). It will probably take the present NHS management until the end of this decade to get to grips with running the service. Rather than force managers to become familiar with medicine, consultants are forced to become involved in management, in a capacity that requires them only to take the blame for failures.

The new reforms have created the need for a vast number of managers in the NHS. Practice managers have become necessary in order for GPs to get to grips with fundholding and its necessary financial and information management. To support directorates within Trusts, co-ordinators, team leaders, assistants, secretaries and clerks have had to be employed. To monitor contracts with health authorities, other providers and GPs, marketing executives, sales personnel, etc have become a necessity. As a result of all this, the NHS has now become seriously overmanned. There have been 30 000 new managers employed in the NHS since 1990 at a cost of over £500 million per annum; there are only about 15 000 consultants. Previously, this money would have been spent directly on patient care. Consequently, while the managerial class expands, the professional classes are shrinking in number (Figure 4.2). Many hospitals are operating year on year on limited and inadequate budgets, so that beds, operating sessions, etc are closed from time to time to save money, leaving consultants idle.

To make the new reforms work, the NHS management had to be invested with formal authority to override professional authority around which the service was previously organized. Consequently, many managers were political appointees recruited primarily to implement government policy. The few recruited from within the NHS were either non-medical professionals, those whose clinical careers had effectively come to an end or those who had personal animus against the 'consultant class'. The new order has resulted in personal gratification for those who had previously been unsure of themselves but were now empowered. Consequently, NHS management has developed a whole new culture and language alien to the health service. In spite of the absence of any intellectual justification, the new managers have come to regard

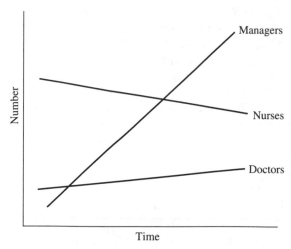

Figure 4.2: NHS staffing trend in the 1990s.

themselves as experts in everything, from treatment of individual diseases to doctors' training. Naturally, the disenfranchised have become frustrated, aggressive and hostile and the cordial relationship and camaraderie that previously existed between managers and professionals have been destroyed.

By all indications, the positive outcome predicted for the new NHS management has not occurred. This is hardly surprising. Firstly, the managerial reforms were politically rather than ethically motivated. Therefore, they inspire very little confidence from professionals. Secondly, there was an implicit, but unjustified, assumption that hospital doctors, unlike GPs, were less competent in management matters than 'professional' managers. Therefore, consultants have been 'functionally' excluded from the Trust's managerial structure. Thirdly, it was assumed that a higher status could be bestowed upon managers simply through enhanced organizational position. This has not happened. Psychologists have long pointed out that managers give orders successfully not because they are inspiring or persuasive but because most of us have been taught from a very early age to obey anyone in authority. In an organization such as the NHS, which depends almost entirely upon human endeavour, leadership derives solely from personal or group skills.

Workers' dissatisfaction and poor performance very often stem from a mismatch between the reality of their position in the organizational hierarchy and their own self-image. In the new NHS, professionals are no longer trusted to do their jobs properly. Instead, they are increasingly being monitored by those who have little practical experience of the job, and changes to working methods are proposed or imposed that often achieve the very opposite of what they are designed to do. Management, customers and politicians now determine standards; each providing a different definition of quality, so that the professional is hard put to please anyone. Unless these matters are tackled head on, and quickly, the NHS as presently understood will almost certainly disintegrate.

The greatest damage being done to the NHS is the shift in emphasis from, and downgrading of, 'professional work', and hence, patient care. Management is the only game in town; it appears to be the sole preoccupation of the new NHS, the only function that is valued. This is most particularly noticeable with nursing, where many tasks, such as bed-making and patient feeding, previously designated 'nursing', are now undertaken by nurse assistants. The result is that nurses no longer have the ear of patients, and no longer know as much about their patients as they used to, since less time is actually spent at the bedside. Practical work (ie on-the-job training), which was the hallmark of nurse training, has all but disappeared. The result is that today's nurses are not as technically proficient as their forebears. Even junior doctors' work has become less 'clinical' and more overtly 'clerkish'.

The leadership debate

The new NHS reforms have left the workforce confused and demoralized. There is a need for leadership to help people cope. The question is who should provide this leadership: bureaucrats or professionals (Figure 4.3)? To some, a leader is a guide, a beacon, a state to which one aspires (type I or *utilitarian leadership*). To others, a leader is the boss, the master, the person in authority (type II or *paternalistic leadership*). The type I leader usually develops from within the ranks, whereas the type II leader is imposed. Type I leadership is achieved or earned and, therefore, commands respect. By contrast, type II leadership is autocratic and feared rather than respected. Type I leadership has followers, while type II leadership has subordinates.

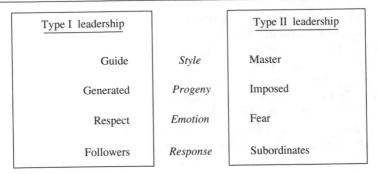

Type I leadership	Style	Type II leadership
Guide	*Style*	Master
Generated	*Progeny*	Imposed
Respect	*Emotion*	Fear
Followers	*Response*	Subordinates

Figure 4.3: Characteristics of the leadership types.

Leadership by managers

For a number of genuine reasons, leadership by management is not acceptable to the generality of the NHS workforce; managers instinctively know this and, hence, their 'lofty' non-functional titles and their preferred physical separation from other workers. Firstly, managers are agents of government, given 'structural' power to control the 'expert' power of the professionals. The general aims of NHS management were to put the clinical trades on an integrated, monitored and subordinate footing. Thus, managers derive their leadership role not from stature, intellectual achievement or professional attributes (ie type I leadership) but from surrogacy (ie type II leadership).

Many NHS workers believe that, as a result of this surrogacy, managers think and act as if the NHS belongs to them. Regardless of the scarcity of resources, they provide themselves with expensive tools (ie computers), while clinicians are asked to make do with whatever is available. They want freedom to act – 'managers should be allowed to manage' – but deny freedom to others. While a manager would 'cling' to his/her assistant, secretary or clerk, he/she berates a surgeon who wants an office or wishes to hang on to his nursing team. While the workforce is required personally to collect data to carry out their duties, managers use other workers to collect data for management decisions.

Secondly, the role of management does not impact directly on medical care. There are no 'visible' concrete tasks. While other health workers 'fetch and carry', managers spend their day at meetings, on the telephone or 'pen pushing'. The manager may control the environment of work but the professionals are operationally independent.

The success of a hospital is not visibly dependent on financial or organizational wizardry but on the skill and expertise of its professional staff. Consequently, management is perceived by other workers as nothing special. The training is not nearly as vigorous as that endured by the professional trades. The function can be carried out by anyone with common sense. All human beings make 'others work for' them; even newborn babies make their parents work for them.

Thirdly, as a result of their surrogacy, managers sometimes appear to work to the detriment of their institutions. Many workers also claim that NHS managers often do not fully understand the business they are supposed to manage. As a result, they appear to operate in a different world from the professionals, and with little or no logic. Decisions are made that are quite often obstructive to the carrying out of professional tasks. Many managers suffer from the 'eureka' syndrome – ideas hit them like a bolt of lightning and they seek to implement them immediately with little consultation.

Leadership by doctors

Unlike managers, doctors rely on their professional expertise as the basis for exercising authority (ie type I leadership). They have no other sanctions and have to rely more on interpersonal skills than any other group in the NHS to avoid the accusation of arrogance. Doctors are the most educated and highly trained of the NHS workforce. Their training is the longest and their career the most arduous. They are, therefore, more intellectually suited to leadership.

Whereas managers are forced to lead, doctors are trained to lead because of their function. The doctor plays the lead role in the delivery of health care and determines the services that the patient receives (Figure 4.4). Consultants feel 'protective' towards other health workers who they regard as a resource necessary for the treatment of patients; hence, doctors are directly involved in their training. In the health care business, doctors own the 'means of production', ie their expertise. Their expertise is not owned by the state or by managers. Therefore, doctors cannot be 'controlled' or forced to comply with managerial edicts like assembly line workers. Doctors are, thus, in the best position to stand up to and resist pressures from politicians. It is they and they alone who can 'protect' the NHS workforce.

Doctors and patients are the reasons for the existence of the NHS. The doctor's primary role is to treat individual patients and his/her primary obligation is to do the best for each one. As a consequence of this, it is alleged that doctors use resources without considering the

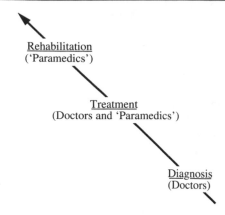

Figure 4.4: Hierarchy of patient needs.

wider implications and are unwilling to accept resource constraints. This is an unfair criticism; the doctor–patient relationship is the engine that drives progress in health care. It is directly responsible for the unrelenting advances in therapeutics and for the fund-raising activities which many doctors engage in. In the course of building professional empires, resources are obtained for associated services – physiotherapy, occupational therapy, chiropody, etc and the institution acquires its reputation.

In the UK, doctors are trained within the NHS from about the age of 20 years, and most spend their entire life working in the service. As a 'junior', the doctor not only works but is obliged to live in the hospital. Consequently, the doctor is exposed to all aspects of hospital life from hotel 'services' to educational facilities. He/she is also in direct daily contact with all sections of the entire workforce from professionals to non-professionals, from managers to cleaners, from laboratory technicians to maintenance staff. Therefore, doctors constantly receive 'feedback' from the entire NHS workforce.

5

'Trojan horses'

Supporters of the management class believe that workers are either too dumb or are incapable of managing their work-place. Managers are necessary, they say, to change and/or reform organizations. For example, if you wish to introduce market forces into a public service like the NHS, you need managers to organize it. The workers themselves could not do it. If you want workers to do their work properly, and diligently, you need managers on their backs, otherwise consultants would spend all their time in their private clinics – presumably this does not apply to the saintly managers who are expected to police themselves. If you want to bring down the price of drugs, call the manager, because doctors cannot choose properly, unless they are given clear options by another group outside of their profession, presumably of more superior intellect. A health service cannot be run by doctors because they have no talent for administration – presumably GPs are not doctors.

How do managers actually achieve this wonder? – by playing musical chairs with the structure of an organization. Managers are obsessed with structure because they are obsessed with power. To achieve anything, firstly, they believe that all workers, regardless of the levels of their skills or of the precedents of traditions or of their worth to the enterprise, should have the same amount of power. Secondly, they believe that managerial power should be at a higher level and that no group should be in a position to challenge the authority of management. It is only by this 'cruciate command mechanism' that change could occur – this is nonsense, of course. When market principles were introduced into education, the responsibility was given to headteachers not to bureaucrats. In order to level down the power of the health professionals, the new NHS management has gone to extraordinary lengths to conceal its real motives.

This managerial obsession with structure reveals a most alarming lack of understanding of the nature of the factors which inform the work of an organization. There are three dimensions to it; structure, process and outcome (Figure 5.1). *Structure* refers to the organizational

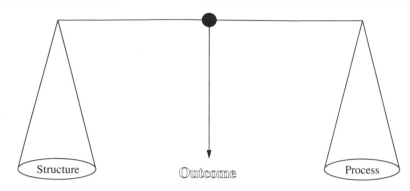

Figure 5.1: Structure, process and outcome.

chart and the location of authority and responsibility. *Process*, which depends very much upon facilities and skills, refers to the performance of tasks, while *outcome* refers to its end-product. To effect change, efforts should be concentrated on *process*. In an organization such as the NHS, in which there is a hierarchy of skills, structure is inbuilt. According to 'free market' principles, the structure is constantly being adjusted; as one or other group upskills, its position in the hierarchy improves automatically. Artificial or imposed structural adjustments are non-motivating and counterproductive; the most highly skilled could simply desert the ship and there is nothing that anyone, short of political coercion, can do about it. Structural 'tinkering' is appropriate only when there is a degree of rigidity and the tasks to be performed are low-skilled, predictable and routinized.

Clinical directorates

The managerial involvement of doctors in the reformed NHS has been largely confined to *clinical directorates*. These have been constructed around clinical specialties, for example, surgery, orthopaedics/trauma, medicine, paediatrics and so on. The usual format is to appoint a lead consultant or consultant manager at the head of the directorate for the purposes of linking the consultant staff with management. The titles of the lead consultant have included clinical director, clinical manager and clinical chairman. In a few institutions, the consultant manager

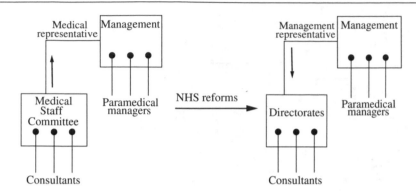

Figure 5.2: The transition from 'our representative' to 'their representative'.

role is formalized with a job description as well as 'managerial remuneration package'. The *Working for Patients* initiative aimed to ensure that consultants were accountable for the use of resources, since their decisions effectively committed substantial sums of money. There were no central directives as to how this objective should be achieved, however. Consequently, different Trusts have evolved different strategies. There is no standard approach; hence, the chaos and muddle with differing types and depth of involvement of doctors.

Whereas in the past the consultants elected one of their number to represent them on the management board, in the directorate system the lead consultant is accountable to the unit's chief executive or general manager (Figure 5.2). In this structure, individual consultants still prescribe treatment and care for their patients but within a 'co-ordinated clinical policy'. Many directorates were created simply because the clinical management structure was a prerequisite for granting Trust status. There was, therefore, in many cases little understanding of the implications of this change. The usual ingredients were a few consultant 'zealots' and 'strong' managerial leadership forming an evangelistic cocktail. The consultant manager was usually part-time in the management role and was appointed by the chief executive, rarely elected by his peers, and the authority vested in him/her in the role was usually ambiguous.

Hospital Trusts have used one of three variants of the directorate formula (Figure 5.3) as a means of securing the participation of the professional staff in the management of the hospital, but the nature of that involvement is more 'apparent' than real. Those who have accepted the roles of consultant managers often do not have adequate

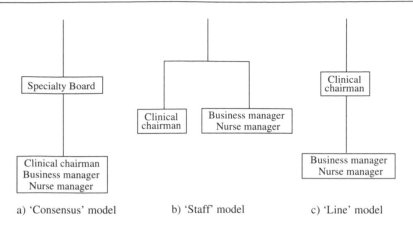

a) 'Consensus' model   b) 'Staff' model   c) 'Line' model

Figure 5.3: Models of clinical directorates currently in use.

or accurate enough information necessary to do their work properly. Yet, they are given day-to-day operational responsibilities. Chief executives have usually not given them a role in strategic planning even though clinicians have a patient-centred approach to matters; even though they are the best placed NHS staff when it comes to identifying the strategic direction their specialty should go. Managers are often reluctant to relinquish central control and have great difficulty devolving to other managers let alone to professional groups who they feel have no skills in management. Managers do not negotiate with clinicians regarding how resources should be used; they simply tell them what they should do. Strictly speaking, since the birth of the NHS, hospital doctors have never had the responsibility for budgets.

Managers would like doctors to look at the impact of their activities in the broader context, not just the patient in front of them. The problem is that the appropriate information is invariably not available for doctors to make these judgements. Often they are provided with highly selected information on expenditure but not much on their individual or collective contribution to the income of the enterprise. This type of information, if available, could, for example, alter perception about a group demanding to increase their numbers at the expense of employing, say, an extra anaesthetist or pathologist, which managers may say is the priority. Information is often released in bits, and then usually bits that pertain only to medical matters. Doctors are rarely, if ever, informed about paraclinical and non-clinical staff affairs. The best way of removing barriers and mutual distrust between managers and doctors is for doctors to be provided with all the information that is available to anyone in the senior management tier.

The directorate structure, as presently operated, mitigates against full consultant participation in management. It is also ultimately unworkable because it is predicated purely upon the desire to control clinicians. There is a belief that, if only doctors were employed in one capacity or another in the management structure, then it would be easy to bring them to heel. This is pure fantasy. The notion of power posits the ability to exercise it in all situations. If power cannot be fully exercised, even if legally possessed, it is nothing but an illusion. In the NHS, managerial power cannot be fully exercised over clinicians because, unlike professionals elsewhere, such as in industry, they are operationally independent. This means that all decisions have to 'defer' to the workers, and management is not in a position to carry out effectively the task with which it was charged by the new reforms. This is why nothing much has changed on the 'shop-floor' in spite of the numerous structural initiatives carried out in the NHS since its inception. The effectiveness of managers is overstated; their employment in the health services is 'supernumerary' and surplus to requirements.

This analysis is not to imply that a directorate structure is not necessary. What is argued is that it is being used to achieve the wrong objectives. The directorate structure is good because it organizes an NHS unit into its constituent functional parts (FPs). Directorates should continue to be headed by consultants because they are the central characters in the provision of the service. However, consultants without managerial duties should be excluded from the command structure altogether (Figure 5.4), since the job of a directorate would be to offer a service to patients and to consultants alike, since they also are, in practice, 'customers' of the NHS.

The 'free market'

The market, a subsystem of the economic system, is the mechanism which regulates the supply and demand of goods and services. It invokes the interplay of a complex of forces. There are consumers presented with many ways of spending their money. There are producers making and selling their wares and persuading others to buy. There is capital; the stock of an organization which it uses to buy equipment and

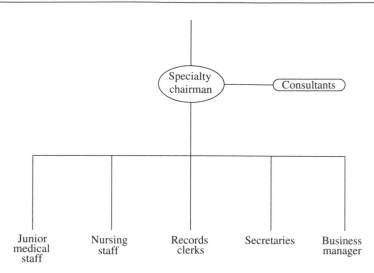

Figure 5.4: Ideal specialty structure.

materials to make its products or its wealth in the form of assets, such as plant and machinery. There is labour, which for a wage offers its skills that are necessary to convert capital into goods and services. NHS free-marketeers believe that a venture can only succeed when its market is completely isolated from the social and political arena. Thus, they believe that the NHS being publicly owned was a ghastly mistake. In the last few years, they have sought to dismantle it and return it to the nineteenth century. However, their notion of the pre-NHS health service is based upon little more than romantic fantasy and falsehood, for it is the failure of the 'free market' that led to the formation of the NHS in the first place.

Pre-NHS assets

On 5 July 1948, the NHS inherited about 3000 voluntary and publicly owned hospitals, with some 500 000 beds. The voluntary (ie private) sector had a minority stake only; numerically, about a third with less than 100 000 beds. There were two dozen or so teaching hospitals which were attached to medical schools and had a fine tradition of high-quality teaching and research. There were numerous small cottage hospitals. Invariably located near the private practices of specialists or close to the residences of benefactors, they were inadequately staffed and resourced. The voluntary hospitals were independent and auto-nomous and each planned its own services for the public as it deemed best. Each was managed by a house governor, chairman or other named officer in concert with an executive committee. They derived their income from charges, voluntary subscriptions and endowments or donations.

The rest of the pre-NHS hospitals, with some 400 000 beds, belonged to local and municipal authorities. They were built under various pieces of local government and public health legislation prim-arily to cater for mental-, poverty-, and age-induced ailments which the voluntary sector neglected. They comprised mainly asylums, sanat-oria, workhouse infirmaries and maternity hospitals; a few were acute hospitals. These invariably enormous institutions, often located away from towns, were usually built as joint ventures between authorities. They were generally managed by medical superintendents directly responsible to the local department of health. The majority were ill-equipped and often they were staffed by GPs and not by specialists. They derived their income from local rates, government block grants, voluntary subscriptions and charges.

As the voluntary hospitals competed with one another, costs escal-ated, threatening the viability of even the prestigious teaching hospitals. The inadequacy of private provision forced the local and municipal authorities to build more and more, and larger and larger, institutions. Two-thirds of the hospitals in 1948 were more than 50 years old and in an unsuitable state to cope with the type of work expected of a modern health service. Many were cramped and uncomfortable for staff and patients alike. The competition between hospitals not only damaged the viability of many, it also created chaos and inefficiency. The desperate struggle for survival led voluntary hospitals to con-template integration (so-called regionalization), as well as to beg for state subsidy.

As a recognition of the chaotic and inadequate state of the hospitals, the Emergency Medical Service (EMS) was established in 1938 to integrate the teaching centres with the service institutions. Resources were pooled, regional co-ordination was established and public health laboratories were developed. As a result of the success of the EMS experiment, it became self-evident that the service could not revert to the pre-war chaos. In fact, these developments had been repeatedly anticipated as the way forward by one committee or commission after another. Even the British Medical Association (BMA) and the Royal Colleges set up a Joint Medical Planning Commission (JMPC) which noted serious deficiencies in the existing facilities and a discrepancy between hospital income and rising costs. The commission found that medical services lagged behind medical knowledge, that quality and efficiency could improve only through the regionalization of the hospital services and the corporate transformation of general practice.

Although the voluntary subscriptions provided up to half of the income of voluntary hospitals – and several million people subscribed – individually, only relatively modest amounts were subscribed. The middle classes were not affluent enough to develop a system success-fully in which premiums could properly pay for benefits as well as for potential risks. The vulnerable groups in society, such as the young, the old, the poor and the chronically sick, were not in any position to contribute financially to the service. On the other hand, the rich only patronized private nursing homes and exclusive clinics. As a conse-quence, the public was forced to contribute the largest share of the fin-ances of the health service. If the market had been able to cope, there would not have been any need for public intervention.

Relatively fewer new hospitals could be built because resources were not generally available for building purposes. Rising incomes did not translate into more resources for the health service, because people had needs other than health, for example, food, clothing, education, housing, etc. Increasing the 'trading income' of hospitals by introduc-ing charges did not guarantee additional benefit to the health service. Funding from elsewhere, especially from the public purse, merely reduced by an equivalent amount once a charge was in effect.

Pre-NHS medical staff

Another outstanding feature of the pre-NHS health service was its scarcity of specialists. According to 'free market' principles, this should not have been so, for the service was desperately in need of specialists. It took the launch of the NHS to stimulate the most rapid expansion of the specialist cadre in history. There were a number of reasons for the pre-NHS state of affairs. Firstly, access to specialist status involved several years of financial sacrifice for the trainee. Secondly, only those with connections or with admission rights to prestigious institutions and who consulted from lavish premises made money. Most worked for local and municipal hospitals and earned a poor wage. Thirdly, specialists lacked control over the conditions of their employment. A significant proportion of their income, for instance, depended upon referrals from GPs. Fourthly, the hospital sector, the only road to a successful specialist practice, was in crisis.

There was in those days a generous supply of GPs which, again according to 'free market' principles, should have driven wages and/or numbers down and diminished their influence. Instead, the GPs were the most powerful group in the pre-NHS era. At the launch of the NHS, they got the best deal and today they are the 'inheritors' of the new NHS. This is ironic considering that, through the BMA, GPs opposed the NHS idea most vociferously and sidelined the initiative by which preventive and curative medicine would have become unified. Primary health centres were to be established containing collective surgeries of GPs in close consultant and administrative relationship with the secondary health centres with a wide range of general and specialist services. Instead, the NHS has been saddled with an inefficient and wasteful tripartite structure, separately administered – ie general practice, hospital care and community care.

There is no such thing as a 'free market' in health, for one way or another, the public always subsidizes insurance-based systems. In the UK, nearly everyone carrying health insurance is registered with a GP and they will still visit a casualty department as and when necessary. Most subscribers have their premiums paid by their employers who set the cost against tax, which is a loss to the public purse. In the USA, administrative costs and issues of morality and social justice have ensured that several groups are excluded from payment and the state has had to provide for them. The NHS costs significantly less than the 'free market' American health service. All in all, financing the health service through general taxation is cheaper than any other method and it allows a rational provision of services. The cost of the NHS in terms of gross domestic product (GDP) is about the same as the public in the UK spends on tobacco.

The early NHS was inadequately funded. Very little additional money was spent on the 1948 reorganization compared with what was being spent on the ramshackle services it supplanted. It is to the credit of those who planned and carried out the change that the immediate objectives were efficiently achieved to the satisfaction of the general public. Unbelievably, within a decade, the NHS was able to provide a universal specialist (ie consultant) service for everyone and in all specialties. The history of the conception of the NHS reflects the failure of the 'free market' in health. In the 1920s and 1930s, in spite of the absence of any restrictions, the private sector had a minority stake only. The voluntary hospitals were in financial difficulty and health provision was inadequate, chaotic and inefficient. Most of the hospitals were in a decrepit state and there was a dearth of hospital specialists, which was reversed only by the birth of the publicly owned NHS.

Empowerment

Empowerment is the instrument with which a 'superior', for example, politicians, may invest authority in or license a 'subordinate', such as managers, to carry out certain tasks. Empowerment is an institutional mechanism for indicating which of two members of a relationship will be superior. It is potential extra power given (ie by a third party) in order to guarantee an *unequal* distribution of power. It is a mechanism for control and co-ordination; easy to use and simple, it does not require subtlety or much understanding. Through it may be imposed orderliness and conformity upon a large organization, such as the NHS, or upon a group, such as doctors.

Politicians, and indeed managers, naturally turn to empowerment whenever there is a likelihood that an intended change will be resisted. It is assumed that empowerment would help the people who have more of it to change the behaviour of those who have less of it. However, empowerment works only if it is acceptable to those deprived of authority as a consequence. For this reason, the outcome of empowerment is most unpredictable. A major difficulty is the high probability of inducing secondary or unintended changes (Figure 5.5). The restrictions that may be necessary to implement empowerment may destroy relationships, frustrate and eventually manifest as resistance and aggression. The recent NHS reforms have sought to empower some groups – GPs, managers and junior doctors – but not others – consultants and

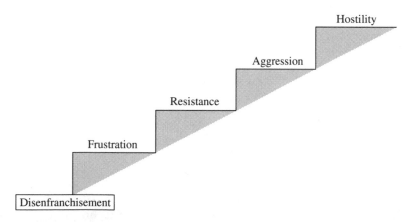

Figure 5.5: The 'empowerment syndrome'.

paramedical staff. The pathological effects are only now just becoming apparent.

Manager empowerment

Manager empowerment is enshrined in the Trust concept, which allows managers exclusively to run our hospitals and other units. Over 30 000 managers have been appointed in the NHS since 1990 at a cost of hundreds of millions of pounds and their numbers are now more than twice that of consultants. While institutional independence, as exemplified by our universities and other institutions of learning, is a good thing, the Trust structure has downgraded, sidelined, silenced and disenfranchised health professionals, including consultants, who are the ultimate providers of hospital care and the most senior employees of Trusts. Consultants are now employed merely as commodities whose main function is to bring in revenue for the Trust. The situation has very important implications which may lead to long-term or permanent damage.

Firstly, professionalism as a calling is being eroded by product line care and attempts to meet real and imagined consumer preferences. Secondly, caring, which is fundamental to competence in medicine, is being violated by productivity and cost constraints. Thirdly, clinical independence, the engine of innovation, is being buried by audit, protocols, quality issues, etc. There is widespread disenchantment with hospital practice with many doctors actively seeking ways of leaving the service. In the current climate, therefore, it is debatable whether hospital doctors are working to their very best.

Professional authority

To reverse these trends, consultants have to resume their leadership role. Their collective professional authority overrides the power of managers and they should use this authority. A stumbling block to this is timidity and it is this that is partly responsible for the present state of affairs. The problem is that consultants are not properly organized or led – 'old fartism' is not confined to the rugby union. The medical profession is almost exclusively governed by those approaching retirement, by self-perpetuating oligarchies and by medical politicians seeking privileges and power. Rather than lead the profession to battle – for the NHS is worth going to war for – they accept 'reforms', no matter how daft the ideas. As a matter of priority, the young and the radical need to be recruited into the chauvinistic bastions of the medical establishment. The rank and file need to be directly involved in the decision-making processes of the colleges and the trade associations.

Just as the unit of primary care is the GP, the unit of hospital care is the consultant. He/she may be helped by his/her junior doctors and by a variety of nursing and paramedical staff to whom some of the work may be delegated. Ultimately, however, the consultant retains full *personal* responsibility for all patients referred to him/her by the GP. It is odd, therefore, that the concept of fundholding has not been extended to the hospital consultant. What is it in the GP's education (or psyche?) that makes him/her suitable for fundholding but the consultant not? Why should GPs run their surgeries and consultants not run their hospitals? It has never been made explicit why hospital consultants are treated differently from GPs by the 1991 NHS reforms.

Unless consultants are in charge again, more and more of them are likely to become 'freelance' and opt out of the NHS altogether. The idea of doctors running hospitals is not new. Until such posts were allowed to atrophy in the early 1970s, some hospitals were managed by medical superintendents. The present situation, whereby consultants are managed (ie controlled) by people who have very little knowledge of medical practice, is not acceptable. Managers do not treat anyone; they have very little contact with patients (see Figure 3.3) and clinical practice is largely independent of them. Yet they have been placed in charge of our hospitals in preference to consultants who have informed insider understanding of clinical priorities. This situation needs to be reversed. Our armies are led by soldiers, the legal system by lawyers; why should our health service not be run by doctors?

6

Prescriptions for the future

At the launch of the NHS, the problems had been to find a secure basis for hospital planning and finance and also to improve the distribution of facilities throughout the country. The tripartite structure was not a bad solution to these problems (Figure 6.1). By the 1960s, the problem had become one of providing services in the most effective and efficient way. The original administrative set-up of the NHS was damaging to the essential unity of medical care and to co-ordination. Therefore, the service was centralized and management was designed to remove the operational difficulties of the tripartite structure.

Since the 1970s, further organizational and managerial solutions have been sought to tackle the new problems of supply being unable to satisfy demand, and spiralling costs. Much of the cost escalation was blamed on administrative muddle and inefficiency, particularly in the hospital sector. Senior doctors were also blamed, rather unfairly, for most of the spending and for being obstructive towards any attempts to improve matters. Today's problems are different again and have to do with overmanning and with protecting the interests of the consumers. The problems cannot be solved by the present 'free market' approach.

Figure 6.1: The tripartite structure.

There is a need to bring the service closer to the customers, as well as to allow the frontline staff a much greater say in managing the service.

Health care systems the world over have survived and prospered on the basis of trust: professionals have been trusted to use the resources allocated to them effectively in the treatment of the sick. By and large, this approach was very, perhaps too, successful. It is apparent that the introduction of management into the NHS has not been any more successful, hence, major organizational changes were introduced into the NHS in 1974 (ie three managerial tiers and 'consensus management'), in 1982 (ie abolition of area health authorities and elevation of districts), and again in 1990 (ie the introduction of general management). The 'trust the professionals' approach is certainly much cheaper than employing an army of expensive, and often ill-informed, managers.

Setting the scene

Particular attention needs to be paid to three matters – *ownership*, *customers* and *facilities* – when seeking to improve the workings of the NHS.

Ownership

With regard to ownership, three groups can make a claim; namely, the tax-payers, the government and the health professionals. In theory, the tax-payers are the shareholders of the NHS. However, they have no means of exercising ownership except at election times. There are no shareholder meetings and no single individual has financial power. On account of the high turnover rate of patients, most of the public demonstrate a transient interest only in the affairs of the NHS. In these circumstances, the public can only exert effective influence if money truly followed the patient.

Since it pays the employees, owns the bricks and mortar and funds the running costs, the government may be said to own the NHS. Consequently, the government determines the framework within which the service operates. However, government has ceded this right to a class of professional managers who are also employees of the service. This arrangement has created its own peculiar problems because the interests of this group coincide neither with those of the customers nor with those of the other NHS employees. The arrangement has created a vacuum in ownership terms, as the recent nurses' pay dispute has shown.

The NHS is different from commercial ventures in that the goods on sale are the skills and sweat (ie the personal properties) of the health professionals. Government and institutions, etc are merely tools that contribute to the efficient delivery of these goods. The ultimate ownership of the service may thus be said to belong to the professional. The health service is acephalous in the sense that managers cannot exercise authority (other than institutional) over the professionals who carry out the most important roles of the organization. Unlike that which obtains in commercial enterprises, the health professionals as a group make decisions concerning the explicit goals of the organization (ie diagnosis and treatment of patients, training and research) and they carry out the decisions themselves independent of management.

Customers

With regard to the *customers*, there are two of them. On the one hand, the NHS provides facilities for patients, whom the health professionals throw a shield around (Figure 6.2), preventing, diagnosing, investigating and treating disease and rehabilitating afflictions. The ultimate goals are to promote health and eliminate disease and disability. There are over 500 million such transactions each year taking place in small groups, often on a one-to-one basis, between individual health professionals and individual 'clients'. The numbers and variety of these transactions are increasing all the time. The reasons for this are threefold. Firstly, as the population now suffers predominantly from degenerative

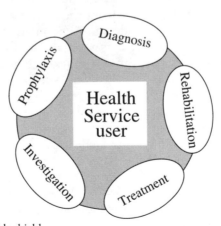

Figure 6.2: The health shield.

rather than infectious conditions, there is a requirement for high-technology medicine. The management of such *facilities* requires knowledge over and above what can be offered by 'general' management. Secondly, people's expectations are high. Only professionals, being aware of the limitations of their craft, can inject a note of reality into the situation. Thirdly, all human organizations have a natural propensity for interstitial growth – upskilling, empire building, new recruits, etc – and the NHS is no exception. Therefore, attention needs to be paid to staff numbers.

Added to this, there are uncertainties. The demands for health care (ie the *activities* to cater for) are unpredictable; the demand for treatment of arthritis, for instance, depends to some extent upon pain threshold and the ability of the individual to adapt to disability. The pattern of ill health cannot be predicted with any certainty; no one predicted the AIDS epidemic, for example. This, predicting the specific activities to cater for in a health service is, at best, a lottery. In these circumstances, purchasing as a form of control is an illusion. Energy should be focused more on creating provisions rather than on first predicting demand and then, as a response, making provisions to match. Services should simply be provided and the customers invited to use them on an emergency basis or, if non-urgent, on a first come, first served basis. The management of such a 'specialized' chaos is beyond the scope of general management.

Facilities

On the other hand, the NHS provides facilities for the health professionals to ply their trade. In this respect, the relationship is akin to that of a market trader renting a stall from the local council. The market trader can carry out his/her trade independent of the council or of a particular market stall and can move his ware from a stall in one town to a stall in another, or from one market to another in the same locality; if he/she so desires, he/she can even operate from private premises. In the same vein, a consultant (as well as any other qualified health professional, for that matter) is able to operate independently of the NHS. This is the whole basis of private practice, where the consultant is a mere 'tenant' renting facilities. Thus, the consultant can be regarded as a customer of the NHS and ought to be accorded the same rights. This should be reflected, as it is in the case of the market trader, in the management structure of the organization. The health professionals should either be totally independent of it or, alternatively, they should be at the helm of it. It is to the advantage of the patient, and of the NHS, however, that the health professionals, particularly consultants, are at the helm.

Health care activities take place in three different sorts of facilities – outpatient, inpatient and community (Figure 6.3). The activities are the same, the 'shopfloor' is the same and the workers are the same, hence, management ought to have the same style. Traditionally, outpatient and inpatient care have taken place exclusively in hospitals, but there is no reason why this should be so. Some of these activities can just as effectively be carried out in the patient's own home or in his/her doctor's surgery. In an efficient system, there ought to be an uninterrupted flow of consumers from one type of facility to the other. A 'provider–purchaser' split will, by definition, interrupt this flow and it will, as a result, be expensive and inefficient. The majority of ailments and measures to prevent and deal with them could be provided on an outpatient basis, but inpatient care will be necessary for some. General practice could offer 'specialist' treatments where the skills are available and casualty (accident and emergency) departments could provide some 'general practice'. Who provides what service, and where, could be left to the professionals to sort out among themselves, since they ultimately have legal responsibility.

The smaller service outlets, such as care centres, GP surgeries and health centres, have traditionally been managed, successfully, by individual GPs and the fundholding concept is a recognition of this. There is no reason to change this management approach, except that health care 'purchasing' should be removed from fundholding. It is an inappropriate function for doctors to perform. Firstly, it alters the way medicine is practised for non-professional and non-ethical reasons. It used to be the practice that GPs investigated their patients as necessary

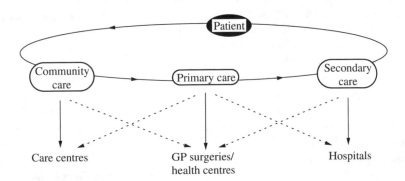

Figure 6.3: The workings of an efficient health service.

before sending them to hospital. With the advent of GP purchasing, patients are frequently referred without investigation, since the cost falls on the GP practice. This results in delay in diagnosis and treatment; and, in some cases, patients are sent to the wrong consultant or clinic. Secondly, 'purchasing' converts GPs from health advisers and helpers to benefactors. There is no other public service in which the 'purchasing' function is completely removed from the customers themselves.

The management of the larger outfits, such as hospital Trusts and community care institutions, needs to be reviewed, otherwise the NHS will never be able to achieve its full potential. Costs are increased because general management is yet another layer of management on top of that which is automatically provided by professionals themselves during the course of their duties. It is self-evident that the advantages cited for primary care would also accrue to the secondary sector, if the health professionals were similarly in charge.

Organization of medical care

An NHS user may obtain medical care from one of three separate and independent 'outlets' or sectors; namely, general practice, hospital care and community care (see Figure 6.1). However, there is no difference in approach between these sectors with regard to the diagnosis and treatment of disease. Diagnosis and treatment are what constitute medical care. Thus, from the point of view of what doctors actually do, the separation of the practice of medicine in hospital from that which takes place in the community is artificial and arbitrary, and to be deplored. This compartmentalization of medical care is, in fact, a modern phenomenon, which is by no means universal. In the UK, it has more to do with history and with a tradition of antagonism between doctors than with administrative convenience.

The basic philosophy underpinning the NHS was the provision of health care for each and everyone through a personal doctor, and the GP was the doctor deemed most appropriate to fulfil this role. Consequently, right from the outset, the GP was made the gatekeeper to the NHS and the hospital sector merely served to meet patients' needs as interpreted by the GP. There was, in addition, a belief that mistakes in hospital practice stemmed from a failure to know enough about people and, therefore, general practice and community care were designed purposely to pick up the pieces. Pre-NHS, local authorities had the overall responsibility for community care, most of which they lost in the NHS reorganization of the 1970s.

Hospital doctors dominate the scene with regard to scientific medicine and the hospital has been transformed from a place where people went to die to a place where life is enhanced and/or prolonged. There has been, in recent years, a technical revolution in hospital care beyond what anyone could have imagined a generation ago. All parts of the body have become accessible to the surgeon, and several can be replaced. Many therapies now use molecular biology and genetic engineering. By contrast, general practice, which has continued to be based upon the 'individual entrepreneur', has been very slow to respond to changes in medical science. Diagnosis is frequently by guesswork and, as a consequence, many illnesses are underdiagnosed and untreated until they become more serious or develop complications. On the other hand, reports from the General Medical Council (GMC) and the defence unions suggest that GPs are not superior to consultants with regard to their knowledge of and feelings for their patients.

General practice is not as cost-effective and/or efficient as it ought to be. Up to a fifth of the population may not even be registered and many more never consult a GP. Accident and emergency (A&E) and out-patient departments (OPDs) often function to take the load off GPs. Many patients who require no specialist care are referred to hospital, and up to half of OPD patients are referred back to GPs after their first visit. Such OPD attenders would have received very little to justify weeks or months of waiting or the bother and expense of attending. OPDs often duplicate general practice work, for in many conditions, such as hernias, varicose veins and grossly osteoarthritic joints, the GP's diagnosis could just as easily be accepted and the patient's name simply added to a waiting list or to a pre-admission clinic rather than receiving an OPD appointment.

There is no comprehensive system of after-care and rehabilitation to match the care offered by either general or hospital practice. The volume of inpatient work increases year on year, but many patients are receiving 'custodial' rather than medical care, because of lack of resources for community care. Patients are left high and dry in the immediate post-hospital period when they are vulnerable to emotional distress and their personal resources may be low. Letters are, in most instances, the only interface between primary care and hospital care, and the only contact between GPs and consultants. GPs often complain about delay in receiving discharge summaries and letters from the OPD, and consultants complain that GP letters are not explicit enough.

In practical terms, GPs are isolated and do not have close contacts with specialists and, hence, with the frontiers of medicine and the tide of technological change. Very little learning occurs from discharge and OPD summaries, since they provide a glimpse only and do not represent the totality of patient experience. A patient is not likely to be seated in front of his doctor on the day the discharge summary is received to corroborate its contents. The negative effects of GP isolation cannot be rectified simply by participating in continuing medical education (CME). Experience shows that a formal and regular clinical attachment to a hospital is the most effective way of raising the competence of GPs.

A GP has no direct access to many of the facilities in the hospital sector that are necessary to make an informed diagnosis, while a consultant has no access at all to GP records that are necessary to provide individualized care. Continuity of care implies a unitary system, yet there is no sharing of information between hospital and general practice, unlike the situation in similar organizations. For example, when one goes into a travel agency, within seconds, the assistant is able to tell you which seats are available on which plane and which room is free in which hotel, even in the remotest corner of the world. The police use similar techniques to call up the driving history of errant motorists. The sector-to-sector communication system of the NHS differs little from that which obtained in medical practice three centuries ago. In the NHS, a similar system to that used by a travel agent or police officers could increase the effectiveness of medical care as well as reduce costs.

In spite of the 'internal market' and fundholding, one sector does not directly influence what happens in another. For instance, there is no liaison with GPs, the primary sources of hospital referrals, with regard to OPD appointments. Hence, there is no relationship at all between the numbers of referrals that are received by a hospital and what the consultants are actually capable of achieving. Referral numbers are not even related to the contract which the provider and the purchaser have entered into. This lack of correlation is a major cause of long waiting times. Conversely, there is no liaison with hospital doctors with regard to the provision of emergency medical cover in the community, especially at night. Hence, the acute services are often inappropriately used by patients, and many GPs overstretch themselves unnecessarily, particularly as the majority of problems end up in A&E departments or in the laps of the consultants anyway. This policy omission is partly responsible for the regular winter bed crises in the UK.

Medical care in the NHS has a tripartite administrative structure (see Figure 6.1) with three different sets of bureaucrats, perks and paper work. This merely serves to increase transactional costs and, as a consequence, the resources that would have been available for direct patient care are wasted on administering it. There is competition between the sectors for resources and pre-eminence. The NHS is pulled three ways as the sectors battle for its soul. A lot of energy is expended by central government and by health authorities in reconciling these three opposing factions. The wedge driven between general practice and hospital medicine by the 'fundholding concept', for example, accentuates the traditional division between the medical profession. For the patient, primary care and hospital treatment should be aspects of a continuum in the management of his/her illness. Hospital and community care are interdependent: what happens in one affects what goes on in the other.

A new approach?

Doctors who work in the community are fundamental to the best practice of medicine. They constitute an early warning system for screening vulnerable groups; they are the only certain means of providing supervision, comfort and advice on an individual and continuous basis; and they provide a sympathetic ear for the emotional and the stressed. Nevertheless, the age of the single-handed practice is over. Medicine as a body of knowledge shifts and expands so rapidly that it is not possible for one man to comprehend, let alone practise, it all. Therefore, GPs should practise in groups of 12 or more, and preferably in a health centre or 'polyclinic' with a panoply of ancillary staff, including social workers, school nurses, health visitors, district nurses, community physiotherapists and chiropodists. The 'named doctor concept' should be retained, however.

With the recent demise of the regional structure and the downgrading of health authorities, community physicians should be moved into GP premises, perhaps co-ordinating the work of some of the ancillary staff, or even as practice managers or directors. Each health centre should be directly affiliated to a hospital or group of hospitals (ie a named hospital concept). To make the best use of the manpower available in the NHS necessitates the cross-delegation of duties; hospital care should be 'coupled' to community care (Figure 6.4). Hospital OPDs in certain specialties, such as dermatology, could be abolished and the consultant clinics transferred to the GP surgery. Consultant follow-up clinics where immediate investigations, particularly radiology,

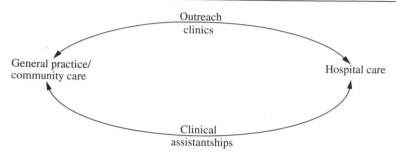

Figure 6.4: 'Coupling' of medical care.

are not required could also be transferred without affecting patient care. At least a third of GPs should have contractual hospital attachments, particularly in OPDs and A&E departments, where they could supplement junior doctors whose roles are currently being redefined.

The separation of medical care into three 'outlets' – general practice, hospital and community – is inefficient with regard to the delivery of health care and the use of scarce resources. To rectify the situation, consultants and GPs need to come together to provide services on a rational basis in order to satisfy the demands for medical care. A highly integrated system of medical care is necessary to improve the dissemination of medical knowledge. The cost of general practice can be reduced by a close association between the hospital and community sectors. Much needs to be done to bridge the gap between primary care and hospital care.

Hospital management

Many NHS employees claim that, in spite of all the new developments in management, hospitals are inefficiently run. Demands are not being met by adequate provision. The budgetary and financial systems in use do not ensure that resources are efficiently and effectively used. Patients not infrequently attend clinics without their case records and/ or radiographs being available. Appointment letters are not sent or are sent late. Necessary equipment is often not available or replaced on time and, when it has been purchased, it is often not properly maintained.

The inability to solve these and other embarrassingly simple problems indicates that all is not well with hospital management.

Hospitals need to organize themselves effectively and efficiently to satisfy:

- *the community* – by providing a satisfactory service

- *the patient* – by providing cure and care as appropriate

- *the staff* – by providing physical and financial security, self-fulfilment and an amiable working environment.

The circumstances in which hospitals operate are constantly changing. Medical technology is improving rapidly and the public is making more and more demands. Strict financial accountability is expected and staff seek job satisfaction and adequate rewards. The new NHS reforms have introduced the concept of 'internal market', fundholding GPs and Trust hospitals. All these changes cause strains which are manifest in low staff morale, frequent criticisms in the media and claims of increased bureaucratization. To these ends, many parts of the present hospital service could benefit greatly from a change in management structure. No systematic answers appear to be forthcoming from the present style of management, however. There are attempts to bring about improvement but these tend to be 'top down' with inappropriate changes imposed from above.

Theory and practice mismatch

NHS hospitals are managed in the bureaucratic tradition and are characterized by division of labour and a hierarchical structure of officials (see Figure 2.3). There is a vertical flow of authority, mainly from the top to the bottom, and a decline in autonomy as you go down the hierarchy. The task of planning a job is left to managers, while the task of doing it is left to the workers. The concept reached its ultimate expression in mass production assembly lines manned by low-skilled workers performing repetitive tasks and organized by a compartmentalized management. This management style has several drawbacks (Figure 6.5) and, consequently, various attempts have been made to democratize the 'shop-floor'. In industry, foremen and supervisors were appointed as the last link in the chain between management and workers. However, nothing much changed, since this development arose solely because management wanted answers to administrative problems and not because of concern for the health of the organization. More recently,

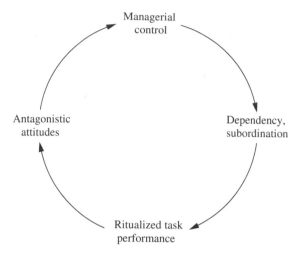

Figure 6.5: The 'post-management' syndrome.

an army of highly paid planners and managers have been employed, much-hyped new management methods have been introduced, and huge computer power has been acquired.

Hospitals do not fit the *bureaucratic model*; for, unlike the situation obtaining in industry, knowledge and qualifications are not concentrated in the middle levels. There are two distinct types of expertise and authority in the NHS; namely, administrative and professional. Administrative authority derives solely from position in the bureaucratic hierarchy, whereas professional authority is based upon expertise, skill and knowledge. The actions of the professional are based upon his/her professional judgement and he/she alone (with the agreement of his/her peers) is in the position to decide. The surgeon, not the hospital's chief executive, decides whether or not to operate on a patient. Naturally, therefore, the professional expects and demands freedom (autonomy) to exercise his/her own judgement and this creates conflict between managers and professionals.

In an attempt to cope with management–professional conflicts, two solutions have evolved in the NHS. Firstly, the rather mechanistic bureaucracy model has been modified by the addition of horizontal lines of communication and control in the form of specialties, work teams and committees. As a consequence, responsibility and knowledge have become more widely distributed as suggested by proponents of the 'organic' model of organization. The dominant aim, however, has been merely to reduce misunderstandings rather than to broaden participation in the decision-making process. Secondly, 'experts', such as medical directors and specialty chairpersons, have been added to the structure and the focus changed from better management to better patient care. These 'experts' have little or no authority, however, and a distinction is usually made between staff (advisory) function and line (executive) function. In practice, the staff section is out on a limb, isolated and playing very little part in the running of the hospital. As a result of horizonal lines of communication, a large part of hospital business is internal rather than being concerned with customers (ie patients). Much energy is expended on improving co-ordination and co-operation between groups, departments or compartments of the bureaucracy. Therefore, a significant proportion of the management staff do nothing but shift pieces of paper from desk to desk. Even the professional staff now spend considerable time on paperwork, which causes resentment.

The hospital as an organization

The hospital as an organization does not fit the bureaucracy model because of its many, often conflicting, goals. Organizations, whether a debating society or an army on the march, exist to assist man in pursuing goals effectively. Therefore, in deciding the management structure for any organization, it is necessary to define the goals and to identify the beneficiaries: mutual societies, such as trade unions and political parties, benefit their members; businesses benefit their owners; service enterprises, such as hospitals and schools, benefit their customers; and the 'public service', such as the police, benefits society. Each type of organization requires a different style of management.

A hospital has two separate and distinct goals; namely, to support the consultant staff who are primarily responsible for providing medical care (ie clinical services) and to provide physical and emotional support for patients (ie patient support services). While the patient support services, which are delivered by unskilled and semi-skilled workers, may lend themselves to bureaucratic organization, the clinical services are significantly damaged by it. Thus, there ought to be two separate but parallel organizations and management within our hospitals; namely, clinical and support businesses. It is for the former sector that a new structure is hereby proposed (Figure 6.6).

As a rule, clinical services are delivered on a one-to-one basis (ie between the clinician and the patient). Since most patients do not

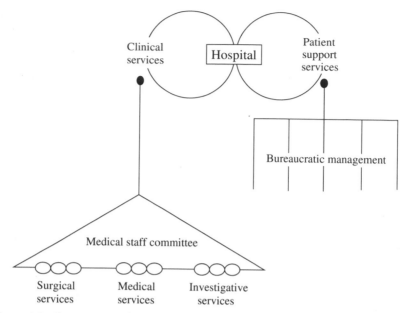

Figure 6.6: Components of the 'hospital business' and management.

require any procedures, a large proportion of the service is provided in clinics which contain little more than a table and a few chairs. Most of the treatment prescribed can be obtained outside the hospital, for example, from the high street chemist shop. Thus, for management purposes, the important aspect of clinical work is that it is done alone or in small groups or teams. The whole edifice of medical law is erected upon the belief that all doctors guarantee the best quality of care for each patient. No other profession offers this guarantee. Each doctor is so indoctrinated during his training, and is taught to value autonomous decision-making, personal achievement and the importance of improving one's own performance. The rewards of major significance are respect and reputation rather than institutional affiliation. Therefore, in general, doctors identify more with the concept of medical care than with the institution and its bureaucratic management.

These features of clinical practice indicate strongly that the management structure of the clinical services should be built entirely around individual consultants. Consultants, like general practitioners, do not need to be employed directly by the hospital. Each consultant could be contracted to a district health authority to provide specified services in his or her field from specified hospital premises. The basic building blocks of the whole service would be modest-sized, specialty-oriented, semi-autonomous, mainly self-managing, budget-holding teams.

There would be separate specialty groups, for instance, surgical, medical and investigative, 'trading' with one another (see Figure 6.6). Each specialty group would comprise related disciplines; for example, the investigative group would include radiology and pathology. The management structure within each group would be based upon an elected chairman (Figure 6.7), whose functions would be to co-ordinate the affairs of the specialty, run the specialty office, negotiate contracts, as well as represent the specialty elsewhere. In order to co-ordinate the entire spectrum of services offered in any particular hospital, this structure may be expanded into a medical staff committee comprising all the consultants. The elected chairman of this committee could act as the 'liaison officer' between the clinicians and the chief executive of the separately managed patient support services, with the hospital board and with the health authorities.

Advantages of the new approach

Several advantages are likely to accrue by removing clinicians from the general hospital management structure. Firstly, managers will be able to use their skills more appropriately and concentrate their efforts on organizing hotel/support services. Managers are not clinicians and, therefore, they have no training in the organization of clinical practice,

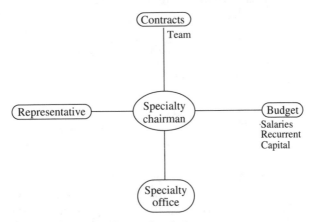

Figure 6.7: Desirable functions of specialty chairman.

yet a significant proportion of their time is expended on this. If this time could be devoted to organizing the hotel/support services, the quality of the facilities provided to patients and clinicians alike would dramatically improve and become similar to that which obtains in the private sector.

Secondly, provider–purchaser negotiations would be directly between the health authority or fundholding GP and the clinician who will actually provide the service. At present, these negotiations are conducted by hospital contract managers and their counterparts in the health authority who have little experience of clinical practice. Consequently, most contracts are based upon arbitrary figures agreed by bureaucrats or dictated by politicians, and this is reflected in the difficulties currently being experienced in fulfilling contracts. These problems would not arise if contract negotiations were based upon the amount of work each individual clinician is actually capable of doing.

Thirdly, areas of responsibility would be more clearly demarcated. Presently, consultants are blamed for everything from outpatient appointment mix-ups to lack of equipment. In the private sector, where the support services are managed separately from the clinical practice, patients know who is responsible for individual aspects of their hospital care. Fourthly, clinical practice would be more personalized as it is in general practice. At present, patients come to a hospital rather than to the clinician who would be responsible for their treatment. This is probably the main reason for the lack of interaction between GPs and consultants. Fifthly, since case records and X-rays, etc would become the property of the clinician or the patient, these items would always be available when required. Finally, as in private practice, clinic and theatre sessions would be more efficiently used because they would be on a book-for-use basis.

Consultant employment

In order to be effective, cheap, accessible to all and of a uniformly high standard, health care has to be provided in an integrated manner. This fact was recognized in the 1940s and, as a consequence, the NHS was created. It was deliberately designed as an integrated system based entirely upon service units (ie districts). The district health authority (DHA), which is responsible for health care in a geographical area roughly corresponding to local authority regions or districts, was the cornerstone of the NHS. Each service unit (SU) consisted of several interlinked establishments or provider institutions (PIs), which provided a number of different services (Figure 6.8).

The old and the new

Each consultant, as the ultimate service provider, was appointed by the SU to work in as many of the PIs as was necessary to complement colleagues within the same specialty. In this way, the clinical divisions (CDs) were formed. In the hospital sector, for instance, members of each CD were charged with 'planning' and 'organizing' district/region-wide services, appointments, training, etc for their particular specialty. Consequently, there was work-sharing between hospitals, which ensured the viability of the smaller PIs, and service-sharing, which ensured that a 'minority' specialist service, such as neurosurgery, was available to the whole population. By contrast, the recent NHS reforms have elevated the institution above the service. This is why the chairman of a Trust could suggest that doctors should place the interest of the Trust above that of patients. Since the Trust structure is based, in the main, not upon service provision but upon institutions (see Figure 6.8), the reforms have 'franchised' services to PIs in a very haphazard manner. As there is no direct, one-to-one relationship between service provision and institutions, in many areas purchasing has become difficult, if not impossible. These post-reform problems have now been recognized, hence, attempts are being made to correlate services with institutions, and a lot of rationalization (ie mergers, introduction of new services, etc) has had to take place, and is taking place.

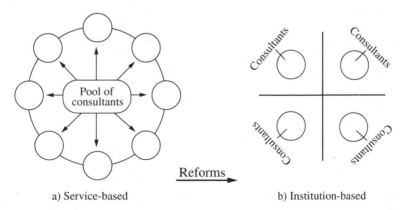

a) Service-based   Reforms   b) Institution-based

Figure 6.8: From service- to institution-based consultant deployment.

On the other hand, by severing the traditional link between institutions, and between institutions and the communities which they are supposed to serve, in many instances (as in London) merely compounds the problems. For PIs are independent competing units, isolated from one another (see Figure 6.8), each contracted for specific services. As a result, services are not only fragmented, aspects are duplicated with attendant unnecessary increase in costs; and the viability of each PI depends upon contract rather than upon use. The SUs have been replaced with purchasers who are not in any position to know what the consumers actually need. This has broken the link between need and provision which previously existed (Figure 6.9); and the 'doctor–patient contract' has been replaced with a 'provider–purchaser contract'. The CDs have been disbanded and, consequently, services can no longer be provided in an integrated manner, even if the purchaser so desires or the nature of the service to be provided so dictates.

These structural conflicts are at the root of the interminable factional struggles that are sapping the morale of the health professionals. It is widely acknowledged that something needs to be done, and some suggest more management, but these conflicts cannot be resolved simply by offering doctors a greater participation in management. A fundamental change is necessary; for, to return cohesion to the service, the NHS will have to revert to being service-based rather than institution-based as at present. Since senior doctors are the ultimate providers of health care, they would need to be at the centre of this new reorganization.

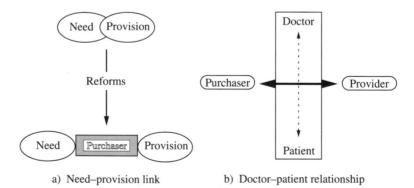

a) Need–provision link   b) Doctor–patient relationship

Figure 6.9: Unpredicted effects of the new NHS reforms.

Consultants within Trusts

When hospital Trusts were created, as a result of the purchaser/provider split, the contracts of consultants were automatically transferred to the PIs. There is reason to believe that this is not the best way of maximizing the use of the consultant resource. There are fewer consultants per head of population when the UK is compared with other developed countries; more significantly so when compared with the United States (US). Therefore, by restricting consultant employment to Trusts, their services are not spread widely enough. This is hardly cost-effective in these cost-conscious times. What could be achieved if Trusts did not have the monopoly of consultant employment is amply demonstrated by waiting list initiatives and by private practice.

The setting up of in-house specialist clinics in GP surgeries shows that a consultant's services do not have to be confined to the four walls of a Trust. The work of a consultant is service-based not institution-based and health care is provided on a one-to-one basis. Consequently, a consultation can take place in the patient's living room and a baby may, for example, be delivered in the mother's bedroom. The institution provides little more than a convenient meeting place between doctor and patient. The recognition of this fact is implicit in the way that primary health care is organized and, hence, GPs have always been independent contractors to the NHS. It is anachronistic that consultants are not employed in the same way as GPs.

At present, the majority of consultants work for more than one Trust. Orthopaedic surgeons frequently have trauma duties at one site, elective duties at another and peripheral commitments somewhere else. Anaesthetists, geriatricians and specialist physicians not infrequently serve several institutions simultaneously. In these circumstances, at present, one Trust is designated as base, contracting the services of the consultant to other Trusts, which then reimburse parts of the consultant's salary, etc to the base Trust. These arrangements task the ingenuity of personnel departments and frequently break down when locums have to be employed or the postholder retires. Thus, the system already acknowledges that consultants do not fit neatly into the Trust structure.

Consultants outside Trusts

A review of the recent lay, medical and management press reveals a very serious rift between doctors and managers. Top NHS managers appear to regard consultants, at best, as the main obstacle to the smooth running of Trusts. Doctors appear to regard management as an irrational process which, at best, is a wasteful and irrelevant distraction from the task of caring for patients. There are two explanations for this mutual antipathy. Firstly, bureaucracy and professional work are incompatible; the former posits control while the latter posits freedom. The reality of life for managers is that doctors cannot be treated like the other employees of the Trust. Since they are the ultimate providers, without them there is no Trust; without doctors, there is no NHS. Doctors are the first drug offered by the NHS to its patients. Therefore, the demand for doctors, and in turn their own demands, will always determine the patterns and priorities of health care. Secondly, management culture and professional culture are incompatible. The unit of concern of the former is the shareholder (ie the government), whereas the unit of concern for the latter is the consumer (ie the patient). The motive of management is profit, while that of doctors is altruism. The main tool used by managers is fiscal or control of resources, while doctors are concerned with improving medical technology, irrespective of costs. These cultural differences result in different thought styles. As a consequence, the two groups belong to different 'thought collectives' and, therefore, no proper communication can ever develop between managers and professionals. Simply involving consultants in 'general' management will not resolve these conflicts. Since the two groups are indispensable to the running of the NHS, however, ways need to be found to organize doctors and managers as parallel groups.

In order to use the few consultants that we have more cost-effectively, it is necessary to take the employment of senior doctors out of the Trust structure. It is possible to do this and still achieve the principles of equity and access which underpin the NHS. It will not necessitate the dismantling of the Trust structure, rather, Trusts will be treated like high street 'retail outlets' for that is what they are in reality. There are potentially three possibilities. Firstly, senior doctors could be organized into chambers or other looser associations, which could then contract with Trusts and/or with purchasers. Although this would have the same effect as the service units, there are a number of problems with this approach. Unlike lawyers in chambers, doctors have no immunity to negligent claims. Therefore, it is likely that the negligence scene would degenerate into American-style claims and indemnity insurance. Furthermore, potentially difficult contractual relationships could arise between doctors and/or institutions, GPs and/or patients. Such cartels may breach the monopoly laws and each doctor in a cartel may be liable for the mistakes of his/her partners.

Secondly, senior doctors could become entirely self-employed as individuals contracting their services to local Trusts. This is what currently obtains in private practice and in the USA. In private practice, the hospital gives the doctor consultation rights based upon his qualifications and expertise. Strictly speaking, there is no direct contractual relationship between hospital and doctor; both patient as well as doctor are customers of the hospital. The doctor is reimbursed on a fee-per-item basis by the patient or his/her insurers. The patient may consult the doctor directly or he/she may be referred by his/her health adviser (ie the GP). This approach does not provide comprehensive care, which is why President Clinton is attempting to reform it. Other disadvantages include costs and the problem of indemnity. The amount of secretarial or 'paperwork' involved for the doctor is often cited as a disadvantage, but this is grossly exaggerated. At present, every consultant involved in private practice runs and organizes this aspect of his/her own practice.

Thirdly, like the GPs in the primary care sector, senior doctors could be employed as independent contractors to the NHS. The 15 000 consultants in the UK would be charged with providing a comprehensive system of specialist care for the entire population. Each consultant would be contracted by purchasers to provide specialist medical services at designated institutions. Consultants could then be organized into self-managing specialties as described above (see Figures 6.6 and 6.7). Within each 'district', members of a specialty in each Trust could be organized into a specialty division (Figure 6.10); a group of divisions

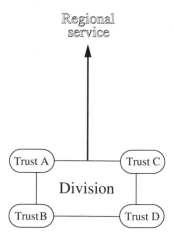

Figure 6.10: 'Divisional structure' for specialties.

would form the *regional specialty service*. This arrangement will not affect the flow of patients to Trusts, since patients will still be referred for specialist treatment in the same way that they are at present. However, consultants will be free to organize their work (and sessions) more effectively, particularly in a way that reflects the levels of demand. For example, in order to cope with the winter flood of fractured neck or femur, elective surgery could be suspended for, say, a month, while every consultant mucked in to deal with the emergency. They would be able to distribute work on the basis of individual talents and not on a rigidly uniform basis as at present; and, as a consequence, contracting would be more specific. The conflicts between managers and professionals will be removed; and patients will again become the main preoccupation of the NHS. This arrangement will restore cohesion to the health service as well as reinforce the principles of equity and access.

7

Training hospital doctors

It is now widely accepted that our system of training hospital doctors (HDs) should be scrapped and that we should start from scratch. Unlike the situation that obtains with the training of GPs, there is no statutory vocational training for hospital doctors. The system has developed piecemeal and it shows. There is confusion and frustration with the organization of the training system which is detrimental to both morale and efficiency. Many bodies appear to be involved in a complex web of relationships with variations between specialties, regions and the constituent home counties. Hence, the organization is not clearly understood by anyone, except by the few 'in the know'.

Objectives

An important matter still to resolve is exactly what the training is for. The aim(s) of hospital training has never really been explicitly stated. Is it to produce specialists or to produce consultants? This is a most important question for the answer to it determines the type, structure and organization of training. Consultants are experts; physicians and surgeons at the top of their profession to whom others may refer their patients for advice. By contrast, a specialist is simply someone who devotes him or herself to a particular branch of a profession. A consultant, being a hospital chief, is much more than a specialist. The training needs of one are different from those of the other.

In many European countries, the specialist is a primary care doctor. In others, it is the entry qualification for training to become a hospital chief. Consequently, in these countries, there are many tiers of specialists. This system is wasteful of resources and ensures that a patient is passed up a treatment ladder from one specialist to another before eventually receiving the appropriate treatment. In the UK, there is direct access to the hospital chief. The NHS is cost-effective because it is a single-tier system of care in which the ultimate responsibility for primary care rests with GPs and hospital care with consultants. Only the UK has an integrated health care system in which comprehensive medical care of the highest quality is provided to every citizen by a network of experts and independent practitioners. In the UK, the requirement is for consultants not for specialists, and this is what we should be training for.

A further problem with the training of HDs that remains unresolved concerns the type(s) of training to adopt. On the one hand, academics, Royal Colleges (RCs) and the Calman initiative favour a formal process of studying, which is informed perhaps by a 'curriculum' or 'syllabus' (ie *studentship*). This has traditionally required attendance at an educational institution. On the other hand, consultants, who, as the ultimate providers of the service, are on the 'shop-floor', favour a less formal process (ie *apprenticeship*), whereby practical skills are acquired consciously and subconsciously. To consultants, the purpose of training is to develop individual and collective abilities to satisfy current and future manpower needs of the NHS. In order for the trainee to achieve effective performance of a range of activities, he/she requires to be trained on the job, since a large component of medical practice is physical.

The distinction between these two approaches to training is of more than academic or semantic interest. Over the years, for example, our medical schools have gone down the former (ie studentship) route. For their pains, however, they now produce doctors who have few or no skills. In industry, 'fast tracking' graduates to senior management positions has proved to be a singularly unsuccessful and wasteful method of producing good executives. Several reasons account for these failures. Firstly, the studentship approach does not allow individual training needs to be identified and satisfied. Secondly, the approach accepts mere exposure to a work situation as sufficient evidence of training, which it is not. Thirdly, trainee expectation of doing an actual job of work during training is usually not satisfied because training is replaced with a seemingly endless and boring collection of information.

A brief training experience offers only very limited advantages. In the United States, many so-called trained surgeons often find that they are ill-equipped and ill-prepared for independent practice and, therefore, they have to go on additional training fellowships. A consultant, being an expert, is by definition trained by practice. This implies experiential learning and, hence, an apprenticeship system is the most appropriate. It also posits several years of learning at the feet of experts, for there is no short cut to expertise. Since people learn and mature at different rates, the duration of training ought to vary from individual to individual.

Organization

At present, the NHS has set up the regional postgraduate system and has set out its desirable functions. However, there has not been established in this system a clear role for the universities and colleges (Figure 7.1). Consequently, there is duplication of effort by regional and collegiate training committees culminating in the absurd situation whereby each has its own clinical tutor carrying out similar but separate functions within the same postgraduate district. These committees need to be rationalized and the two systems merged.

The regional postgraduate system should be consolidated and organized into autonomous institutions along the lines of universities and other institutions of higher learning. A network of local postgraduate centres (PGCs) headed by individual directors or principals should constitute a regional postgraduate medical college (RPMC) or a deanery (Figure 7.2). The RPMC should organize the training schemes while the PGCs organize the teaching programmes. There are enormous advantages to this. Firstly, the chain of command will be visible to every one. Secondly, a satisfactory relationship will at last be established between service and education with a 'right' to time for

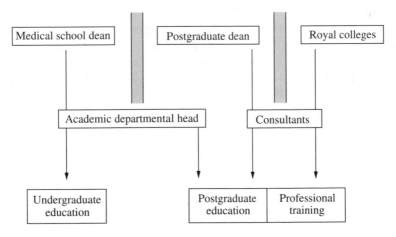

Figure 7.1: The three 'blinkered' hospital trainers.

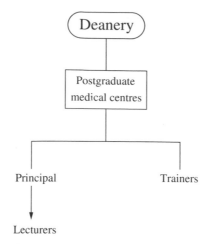

Figure 7.2: The postgraduate medical 'deanery'.

education guaranteed for both trainee and trainer. Thirdly, consultant appointment will become part of a more rational system than exists at the moment.

Funding

The pattern of funding of hospital training has developed in a piece-meal fashion rather than as a result of systematic planning. There is division of financial responsibilities for medical education: undergraduate training is funded by the universities and postgraduate training by the NHS. The guidelines deliberately exclude direct payment to senior doctors for training their juniors, as these activities are regarded as inseparable from patient care and from undergraduate teaching. To this end, there has been an unwritten contract between trainees and consultants – in return for training and mentoring, the trainee looks after the consultants' patients. This contract is being unilaterally broken by Calman and by the junior doctors' hours deal. The consequences are potentially disastrous for training and some means will have to be found to recompense consultants; perhaps by giving them protected teaching times and by making certain junior posts supernumerary (ie service posts).

Trusts (and health authorities) contribute financially towards postgraduate courses organized by universities and colleges, towards the regional postgraduate dean system, as well as honoraria for clinical tutors. Other responsibilities include study leave, examination and travel expenses, upkeep of postgraduate centres and other educational facilities. At present, in spite of the establishment of 'protected funding and educational contracts', expenditure is determined in the light of other commitments. Consequently, there are marked differences in the provision of postgraduate medical schemes between the regions. From the information currently available, the cost for hospital training has been estimated to be about £400 per annum for each junior hospital doctor. This contrasts sharply with approximately £4000 per annum spent per GP trainee from funds directly supplied by the Department of Health (DoH). To achieve the same level of professionalism that characterizes the GP training system, the funds available to train each hospital doctor have to be substantially increased and should be derived directly from the DoH. The funds should be separate from service funds.

Co-ordination

There is a need for a central mechanism for defining the quality and content of training (Figure 7.3). The General Medical Council (GMC) subserves this function in respect of undergraduate education and with

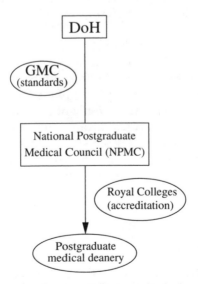

Figure 7.3: A unified structure for postgraduate medical education.

regard to the training of pre-registration House Officers (PRHOs) and Senior House Officers (SHOs). The role of the council should be extended to include the development of standards for each specialty as it has done for the undergraduate course. The council could use the same tenets as those used to develop GP training, ie the content of training to be specified, trainees to be fully supervised and the experience gained to be assessed.

The GMC, as presently constituted, is a judicial, regulatory body; it cannot perform the double function of setting standards and implementing them. A strong framework with statutory powers and recourse to public funds is necessary to implement the standards to be laid down by the 'enlarged' GMC. A central co-ordinating body (ie a national postgraduate medical council, NPMC) is needed to ensure that facilities for training are available, adequate, organized and well funded. This will ensure efficient deployment of available educational and service resources. This organization should be independent and be made responsible for monitoring all training matters. Its membership should include all organizations concerned with medical education and the provision of medical care. There is a need for a clearing house for general information about training. A central mechanism is required in order to reconcile the service needs of the NHS with the training needs of the junior doctors, and to create a rational career structure geared to a vocational training programme, which begins at the PRHO grade. The NPMC is ideal for fulfilling these roles of co-ordinating and focusing the responsibilities of several interested organizations.

The Royal Colleges (RCs) have formed joint committees on higher specialist training (JCHST) because they recognize that certain functions require centralized action. An intercollegiate inspectorate system exists for certain non-consultant posts. This needs to be extended to include all non-consultant posts in all hospitals. There is, at present, very little information on educational attainments and training experience of several thousand SHOs and registrars. This task should be delegated to the RCs. It is unlikely that the colleges will have the financial or human resources to carry out this enlarged task. Therefore, official recognition needs to be given to allocating funds specifically for accreditation.

The role of academics

The question of who should be in charge has been another matter that has been fudged over the years and this has had a detrimental effect on the training of hospital doctors (HDs). Hospital training will only achieve the highest quality when it is organized separately and independently from our medical schools (Figure 7.4). Consultants should be in total charge as postgraduate deans or provosts, principals or directors of PGCs, local training organizers and tutors. Training programmes rely entirely, and always will, on consultants as teachers. Being in practice, consultants know exactly what is required. At the basic level, most trainees and most consultants have the same goals and aspirations.

For a number of reasons, academics are totally unsuited for organizing and running hospital training. Firstly, their primary loyalty is to their employer, the university, and not to the NHS. Whatever they do is motivated by this circumstance. Secondly, they have enough on their plates with research, undergraduate teaching and other university matters. Their numbers are small and, consequently, they are overstretched. Thirdly, and most importantly, their recent record with undergraduate training has not been a resounding success. They currently deliver 'unfinished products' to our hospitals after four to five years of structured, ritualized teaching. On qualification, nurses nurse, physiotherapists treat, but house officers attend 'finishing schools'; once upon a time, our medical schools turned out GPs. Fourthly, there is nothing special in the training of academics which equips them better than consultants to organize and deliver training.

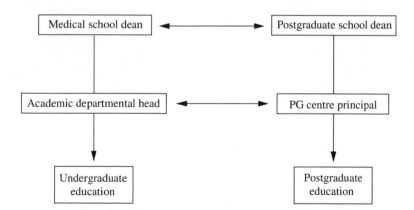

Figure 7.4: Two parallel 'deaneries' for training in medicine.

Methodology

As the millennium approaches, the service commitments to be fulfilled by hospital doctors have yet to be reconciled with their training needs. The traditional open-ended approach favours service in place of training, while the Calman approach favours training in place of service. The former approach is not acceptable to trainees, while the latter is not acceptable to consultants. One solution is to have two sets of junior doctors; one training, the other not. This, in effect, is what is happening at present, but the way it operates is now widely accepted to be unreasonable and unjust.

The other solution, treating all junior hospital doctors the same, is to have periods of purely academic training separated from, and sandwiched between, periods of service or on-the-job 'vocational training' in a continuum (Figure 7.5). To this end, the training could be in five stages spread over an eight year period (Figure 7.6). After five years of university education, the newly qualified doctor deserves a rest from formalized teaching. Therefore, the first two years after qualification should be devoted entirely to service and designed to familiarize the new doctor with hospital practice in both teaching (TH) and general (GH) hospitals. The trainee would be expected to provide

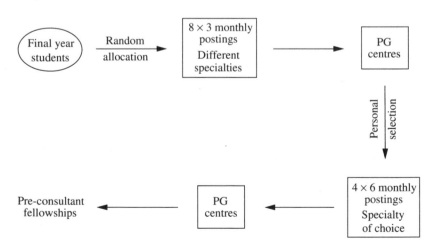

NB: when fully operational, one-third of trainees in 'classroom', two-thirds in 'service'.

Figure 7.5: A training continuum for junior hospital doctors.

Stage	Duration (years)	Service	Education
I	2	Full-time	Vocational
II	1	'On-call'	Didactic
III	2	Full-time	Vocational
IV	1	'On-call'	Didactic
V	2	Full-time	Vocational

Figure 7.6: A five-stage hospital training programme.

basic medical care for patients, particularly on the wards. The academic content of this period of training could be enhanced by periodic lectures and demonstrations.

The third year post-qualification should be in the form of a full-time foundation (ie basic sciences) course in a TH with all-day lectures, practicals and demonstrations. The only clinical content would be *on-call* commitments to reduce the number of hours worked by the service or 'jobbing' trainees and clinical attachments to 'shadow' consultants, as required in the curriculum. There should be an examination at the end of the year – anyone who fails should perhaps have a year added to their training at the next level as a penalty. This third year could be spent, if the trainee prefers, as two years in a lectureship in an academic department pursuing basic research. A thesis would serve the same purpose as the formal examination. At the end of this training period, the trainee would be expected to choose his/her specialty.

The fourth and fifth years of training should be devoted to service in a capacity similar to that of current registrars in a district-wide rotation involving teaching and general hospitals in the specialty previously selected by the trainee. The academic content of this period of training could be enhanced by logbooks, distance learning packages, periodic lectures, etc. The sixth year should be spent in the classrooms on a very detailed full-time specialty course. The only clinical content would again be on-call commitments to reduce the number of hours worked by the 'jobbing' trainees and clinical attachments to 'shadow' consultants. There would be a clinical examination at the end of this period of training – anyone who fails should perhaps have a year added to their training at this level. The whole of the first four stages of training of each HD should take place within the same postgraduate region/district. All trainees should be registered 'students' of the local postgraduate centre. The previous set-up, whereby a doctor moves from one area of the country to another in search of a training programme, is totally unjustifiable.

The final two years of training should be pre-consultant, 'preparatory schools' in THs and could be in the form of six-monthly specialty fellowships in at least two areas of the specialty. It is doubtful whether an 'exit' examination at this stage will serve any useful purpose. The in-service training periods (ie years 1, 2, 4 and 5) could be lengthened as required to accommodate those who, for one reason or another, desire flexible or part-time training, or those whose progress in acquiring necessary skills is adjudged to be 'slow'. In this respect, as in the training of airline pilots, numbers should be set (ie explicitly) for procedures, clinic runs, etc, which a trainee is expected to have carried out under supervision before he/she is accredited or accorded the status of consultant.

8

Getting more for the money

There are three fundamental ways by which the NHS could get more for its money. It could:

1. reduce *costs* – fixed and variable

2. increase *productivity* and/or

3. increase *prices*.

Reducing costs comes first because 'money saved is better than money earned', and it is more certain. The NHS, being a public service, there is very little scope for earning significant amounts of money. *Fixed costs* or overheads do not vary very much in relation to activity. Rents, rates, salaries, fixed interests or dividends, etc have to be paid regardless of whether or not anything is produced or any patient is treated. Furthermore, these costs will not alter as a result of change in activity. In contrast, *variable costs* vary with the level of activity. If, for example, output increases by 10 per cent, expenditure on raw materials for making the goods and the extra labour required will also increase by about 10 per cent.

As output increases, unit costs decrease because fixed costs are divided between the units of production. For example, if the output is 500 units, each unit will bear a 1/500 of the fixed cost; with a production level of 5000, each unit bears 1/5000. Provided the variable costs are not too high, increasing productivity will reduce costs and increase profit or surplus (Figure 8.1). Medicine is a hands-on, physical endeavour, however; there is a limit to what each individual doctor or nurse can physically achieve. Therefore, to increase productivity substantially, additional professional staff will be required which will push up costs; to compensate, the numbers of non-professional staff will have to be reduced.

In the NHS, approximately 70 per cent of the expenditure is on staff salaries, 20 per cent on fixed costs and only 10 per cent is consumed directly by patients. In these circumstances, it may be assumed that

Figure 8.1: The cost–activity curve.

more significant savings are likely to be made by reducing staff than by reducing the consumption by patients. However, this does not appear to be the accepted wisdom by the powers that be. Hence, a large amount of managerial, and political, energy is devoted to reducing patient costs. Even if all medical interventions were appropriate and cost-effective, the effect on overall costs will be minimal.

Rationing

For decades now, opponents of the NHS have predicted its imminent collapse citing in evidence demographic trends, rapidly advancing medical technology, insatiable demand and ignorant doctors. They visualize an ageing population, plagued with chronic ill health, kept miserably alive for the hell of it by medical mavericks. The solution they propose is rationing by techniques, such as waiting lists, managed care and evidence-based medicine. Rationing implies a deliberate denial of treatment. It is often justified on the assumption that health care costs are irreducible. The NHS is an open-ended commitment, but what can be achieved and the availability of medical care depend upon a variety of factors. The important factors on the supply side are the numbers and skills of the professional staff, the facilities and their distribution and finance. The important factors on the demand side have to do with access and eligibility, the prevalence and types of diseases and the age distribution of the population.

Waiting lists

In the NHS, patients have access to all possible medical interventions but, apart from emergencies, there is no absolute right to treatment, or at a time of one's choosing. The timing of treatment, and its availability, depend upon the doctor's discretion, hence waiting lists (WLs). A WL is not necessarily rationing, however, for it only requires the patient to wait his/her turn. True, it may arise because there is not enough capacity – consultants, sessions, facilities, etc – in the system. In many specialties, consultants, who number less than a few hundred, are expected to provide specialist care for 56 million people. In such a circumstance, a WL is unavoidable. A WL is not necessarily a bad thing either, for it allows individual surgeons to prioritize their services. The main disadvantage of a WL is that it is discriminatory. As a consequence, what is available for one patient is not available for another equally deserving patient, and there is also variability from one part of the country to another. As has become apparent in recent years, WLs are open to political manipulation.

Managed care

Managed care restricts entitlement to what has been decided as being affordable by managers. It defines 'medical necessity' solely on the basis of managerial rather than professional judgement. This method of rationing results in à la carte medicine with managers and insurers picking and choosing on the basis of statistical quirks. What is deemed fashionable may depend upon no more than the way a study is presented or upon the clout of the proponents.

Managed care shifts authority from 'players' (ie health professionals) to 'spectators' (ie managers), so that managerial decision overrides clinical needs. Treatment becomes a game, a sort of tug-of-war between clinicians and managers, with the patient having very little say. Differences in opinion between managers and clinicians would lead to an erosion of the doctor's authority and, as a result, his/her effectiveness. Managed care is insensitive and tends to generate dissatisfied customers. Patients lose their medical 'advocates' because the appeals procedure is usually time-consuming. The system is corrupting because only doctors who toe the line are favoured. It is usually bypassed by the rich and powerful which is why there was no outcry when the Queen Mother had her hip replaced at the age of 95. It generates disaffected people and is, therefore, open to media manipulation for individual cases.

Evidence-based medicine

There is nothing new in the concept of evidence-based medicine (EBM). It is as old as medicine itself. One group or another is always setting itself up as custodian of the Holy Grail of best medical practice. Once they told us that bleeding and leeches would cure all ills. In medicine, there is no absolute truth; what is regarded as the best treatment today may be regarded with mirth tomorrow. Consequently, medicine advances in leaps and bounds. There is no room for humanity or individuality in EBM. Since an illness has both physical and psychological dimensions, clinical effectiveness does not necessarily translate to patient satisfaction. A fracture of the wrist may be successfully treated with a simple bandage but, for comfort and pain relief, most orthopaedic surgeons would rather use a plaster cast. Rigid adherence to guidelines (the leeches syndrome) is not always best for the patient or cost-effective in practice.

Guidelines

Proponents of managed care and EBM believe that they are best disseminated via guidelines or protocols and/or by continuing medical education. There is a lot of evidence to suggest that guidelines do not assure optimum care, however. Since there is no absolute truth in medicine, treatments come and treatments go. A guideline imposes control, so inhibits initiative and fossilizes thought. Advances occur in medicine precisely because there are no guidelines. Guidelines coerce and professionals cannot be doing their best if they are being coerced (see the history of Soviet medicine). Traditionally, the way things are done in medicine is to persuade, not coerce. If any group is convinced of its cause, it should inform and convert, rather than issue guidelines.

Clinical trials, upon which guidelines are based, are often badly conducted and evaluated. Furthermore, they are open to abuse and peer review provides no guarantee. Illness is an individual thing; the manifestation of a particular pathology may depend entirely upon the patient's innate constitution. If a guideline were to cover all eventualities, it would be no better than a standard textbook. If it did not cover all eventualities, some patients will be receiving sub-optimum care. What is the purpose of several years of university education, postgraduate training and a lifetime of experiential learning if consultants are reduced to the status of Chinese barefoot doctors? Novices paint by numbers; experts do not. A consultant cannot be called a specialist, if he/she needs guidelines to practise his craft.

Continuing medical education (CME)

Continuing medical education is likely to be made compulsory by the government or the Royal Colleges and written into future contracts. Consultants who refuse to participate may be forced to leave clinical medicine altogether or lose merit awards, teaching status and/or College membership. The form this is to take and who should be in charge has not yet been thought through. Some believe that the scope should be all embracing and should include management and communication skills and that it should not simply be a means of remedying inadequate performance.

The principal danger of CME lies in the fact that it is open to abuse. Through it, consultants could be blackmailed by all sorts of people or groups. Managers, for example, could use it to hire and fire. Lawyers could use it to great effect in negligence cases. No evidence has yet been adduced to demonstrate that formal or structured CME improves, or for that matter, has any effect on, professional competence. This is, in part, because the educational content of most CME is poor. Often, the same set of lecturers are recycled from meeting to meeting, from course to course, and with the same poor materials. Many local meetings provide little more than an excuse for socializing or catching up with old friends and gossip.

While it may be easy for consultants in teaching hospitals to meet CME targets, consultants in two- or three-man practices in district general hospitals will have problems. A significant amount of effort is required for CME which will take consultants away from the work for which they are paid by the public. Patients want to consult experts, not professional students. Experience, volume of work and motivation are what make a competent doctor. All these often touted methods of bringing doctors up to date are mere tinkering only. They are unlikely to have a significant impact on costs.

The clamour for managed care, EBM, CME and guidelines, etc presupposes, without much evidence, that doctors do not know what they are doing, and why they are doing it. Intelligent beings do not spend their lifetime unquestioningly, day in day out, week in week out, and year in year out, not knowing what they are doing. It is not to be deplored that some doctors still practise techniques they learnt decades ago, for experience is the best teacher of all. Good medical practice is based upon personal experience acquired over a number of years, not upon fads, journals or someone else's expertise, irrespective of the intellectual credentials of the source. Consultants know that some treatments are 100 per cent effective and others rarely so. With less effective treatments, more information is sought to determine whether this is a personal failing or whether there can be improvement. With new treatment, one either participates in personal 'clinical trials' or awaits the results of those conducting such trials formally. This is how advances are made in medicine, ie from the medical profession as a whole. Individual experience, not prospective randomized clinical trials, saw the back of leeches and bleeding as the panacea for all ailments.

The road to improving competence lies in integrated, collaborative work within a 'specialty division', ie a group of consultants of the same specialty providing a service as a unit to several institutions within a catchment area. A novel approach would be to organize periodic consultant swaps or internal 'exchange programmes', whereby a consultant in a teaching hospital would spend perhaps a month, every couple of years or so, working in a neighbouring district hospital, while a consultant in a district hospital could do the same in reverse. This could serve to alleviate the 'boredom factor' which frequently afflicts the matrix organization of medical care. Individuals within such groups will learn together and from one another faster than through CME or guidelines.

Which 'internal market'?

The *Working for Patients* proposals for securing and providing services envisaged an 'internal market' in which the health authorities (HAs) purchased services on behalf of their population from provider units such as Trusts (Figure 8.2). There are potentially two distinct and separate types of markets. In one (type I), the patient is treated only through 'contracted' providers, while in the other (type II), the patient receives treatment from any provider and his/her health authority later reimburses the provider.

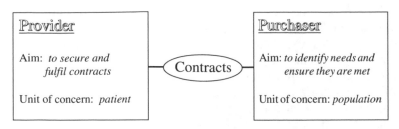

Figure 8.2: The provider and purchaser roles.

Type I market

In the type I market, some or all of the health care needs for a defined number of potential patients are purchased on the basis of contracts. *Block contracts* force the providers to treat as few patients as possible as well as limit the level of service to the minimum specified in the contract. *Cost-and-volume contracts* encourage providers to select cheaper cases as well as minimize the level of service to individuals. With block contracts, the provider carries the risk, while with cost-and-volume contracts, the risk is carried by the purchaser, who still has to provide additional funds if demands exceed planned levels. Consequently, in practice, purchasers insist on mixed contracts and also offload costs onto other services, such as community care. Hence, the overall health cost to the nation is not significantly altered.

There are many other problems with the type I market. Firstly, the contracting is inherently unsound. It is near impossible to devise a sensible contract for services such as general medicine which cannot be 'packaged' like elective surgery. If a contract is made for 100 hip replacements, the 101st patient could be persuaded to wait for the next contract. By contrast, the 101st patient of a contract for the treatment of 100 heart attacks still has to be treated or he will die. Furthermore, it is not possible to assess the health needs of a population accurately. The prerequisite data are not available for any population in the world. At present, information from local people, illness and mortality statistics and annual reports by Directors of Public Health are used to assess needs. On the other hand, the health needs of a population are constantly changing. For example, no one foresaw the AIDS epidemic until it happened.

Secondly, contracting is damaging to the ethos of the NHS. In the past, priority setting, although initiated by politicians nationally, was carried out locally following agreement between the health authorities and the professionals (Figure 8.3). Consequently, health planning was an integrated process involving preventive and curative medicine as well as rehabilitation. What will happen now when a need arises for which there is no provider? The particular service may even have been forced to close by reorganization following previous contracts. The annual contracting ritual poses planning problems for providers and jeopardizes future advances in medicine. What about the national character of the service? One lot of purchasers can legally exclude whole categories of treatment which others elsewhere include.

Thirdly, the transactional costs in the NHS have risen sharply since the introduction of the reforms. The managerial cost for 1992 was over £550 million and it is likely to be significantly higher still year by year. To support their purchasing functions, the HAs have had to employ staff with considerable managerial expertise. Assessing the needs of the population has required surveys of local people and similar exercises by Directors of Public Health in producing their annual reports. Provider units have also had to set up new contracting departments, all fully equipped with the latest computer technology. This money could have been spent on treating more patients or improving community care.

Finally, although the HA plans and contracts for services it identifies, the decision as to which specific individual actually receives the service is made by the customers (ie patients) and by their advisers (ie GPs). The GPs are independent contractors, not agents or employees of the purchaser, so that their duty is primarily towards the patient and

Figure 8.3: The pre-1989 mechanism for deciding priorities.

not the purchaser. There is no relationship at all between contracts and the pattern, rate or volume of referrals to the providers. Therefore, it makes very little sense for the purchasing function to be carried out by HAs. If HAs are to continue to be responsible for purchasing, then they should also be responsible for referring individual patients to the provider. Having said all that, it is difficult to perceive of the scenario in which the purchaser, unless a GP fundholder (GPFH), could refer patients individually to the provider.

Type II market

By contrast, the type II market, which is the closest to a truly free market, is favoured by health insurers and by non-NHS or private providers. It transfers initiative from bureaucrats to the market customers (ie patients) and their advisers (ie GPs). In the NHS as presently constituted, the patient (at least, of a non-fundholding GP) is supreme. Like a student seeking higher education, he/she is free to choose which doctor to treat him/her and in which hospital he/she wishes to be treated. The GP is his/her adviser and not the gatekeeper to the NHS. In these circumstances, the purchasing function of the HAs is an anachronism. If it has any role at all, it should be similar to that of local authorities (LAs) in education. The LA cannot tell a student where to go or what course of study to pursue. Similarly, the HA should not be in a position to determine access to hospital care.

The type II market has several advantages and it is the only means by which the hopes embodied in *Working for Patients* can be delivered. Firstly, it will introduce genuine competition into the NHS, since money would truly follow the patient. Secondly, it will encourage individual providers to innovate and develop as it has done for fundholding general practices. Thirdly, by relieving HAs of their purchasing function, they can concentrate their efforts on preventive and social medicine, which is presently in an appalling state. In the new structure envisaged for the NHS (Figure 8.4), hospital services would be divorced from the HAs and be supervised by a new body, the 'Trust' authority (TA). The TA would have a similar function to the University Funding Council.

Three objections have been raised concerning the type II market; namely, unpredictability of income for providers, high costs as providers seek to maximize incomes by inflating demands and lack of a role for HAs. These objections can be overcome by the method that is selected for financing providers. In the type II market, the provider may be reimbursed retrospectively, ie after the service item has been

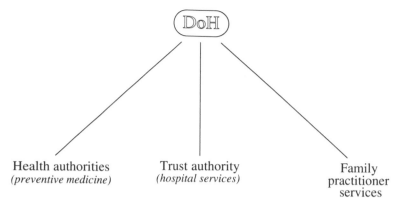

Figure 8.4: A functional structure for the NHS.

delivered (*type IIa internal market*). To reduce costs in the private sector, the level of benefits to which individual patients are entitled is published and the BMA also published a guideline of fees for doctors, which has had to be withdrawn for legal reasons. Although not enforceable in law, the providers generally charge within these guidelines, and yet they have been able to make profits for their shareholders. In theory, the provider does not know beforehand the volume of trade and, hence, cannot predict income and cannot plan ahead with any degree of confidence. In practice, however, NHS providers under the 1990s regime are no better at predicting demands than private hospitals.

To ensure that incomes are predictable and that HAs have a role, the provider may be reimbursed prospectively, ie before the service item has been delivered (*type IIb internal market*), using pre-agreed tariffs, content and volume. The universities and local authorities are funded in this manner and there is no reason why provider units should not be so funded. There are data from elsewhere, particularly the USA, to show how the type IIb market can be used to reduce escalating medical costs.

Block grant

In the university set-up, each year the government provides a block grant to each institution (ie provider) based upon the recommendations of a funding council. The members of this body are independent and are appointed by the Secretary of State. The grant is calculated and identified as teaching or research. The calculation for the teaching component is based upon the expected number of students within each subject category, the level and mode of study and whether students are full-time or part-time. The calculation for the research component is more complicated. This 'upfront money' amounts to some 80 per cent of each university's recurrent expenditure and a large proportion of the capital expenditure. The institution is relatively free to spend it as it wishes.

In addition to the block grant, each student brings with him/her a 'tuition fee', provided as a grant by his/her local authority (ie purchaser). These fees are standardized and the monetary values are determined by the type of course for which the student is enrolled. There are three price categories: non-laboratory-based courses (category 1) are priced less than laboratory-based courses (category 2), which in turn are priced less than clinical-based courses (category 3). The tuition fees allow institutions to expand into higher incomes. Apart from agreeing tariffs, neither the government nor the local authority has much say in this market. Each university operates under a Royal Charter or Act of Parliament, which guarantees it complete academic and managerial freedom. The university decides which and how many students to admit, and what and how to teach them. It decides which degrees to award and under what conditions. Prospective students select by themselves which institutions they wish to attend.

Translating this concept to the hospital sector, at the beginning of the year, each hospital would receive a block grant as determined by a central health funding council (Figure 8.5). The grant could be calculated using the same criteria as are currently employed for reimbursing local authorities. In addition, each patient will bring with him/her a 'service fee', previously agreed with the TA in the form of, say, a grant or a 'voucher'. The value of this charge could be based upon a unit of workload regardless of the actual cost. The unit could be OPD visit, inpatient day, diagnostic test, type of procedure or a combination of these. Alternatively, pricing could be based, as in the university system, upon service categories such as:

- I OPD, investigation, follow-up

- II OPD, investigation, once only non-operative treatment

- III OPD, investigation, once only operative treatment

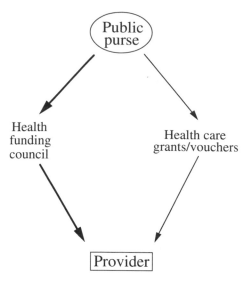

Figure 8.5: Funding of provider institutions.

- IV OPD, investigation, non-operative treatment, follow-up
- V OPD, investigation, non-operative inpatient treatment, follow-up
- VI OPD, investigation, operative day-case treatment, follow-up
- VII OPD, investigation, operative inpatient treatment, follow-up
- VIII accident and emergency
- IX chronic diseases.

Diagnostic related groups (DRGs) which classify inpatients into 'clinically meaningful and homogeneous' groups were developed along these lines. Providers are reimbursed at a set price for each case according to the DRG, but this system is unnecessarily complicated and will eventually prove unworkable.

Demanagerializing to reduce costs

Management doctrines may be classified crudely as efferent or afferent.

Efferent doctrine

The efferent doctrine, which is 'top-down', is favoured by managers and politicians. A 'global' picture is first arrived at following analysis and systematic review and, thereafter, it is broken down into its 'constituent parts', and structures and processes are devised accordingly. Disaggregation is arbitrary, however. Decisions tend to be radical, but the outcome is unpredictable and seldom what is desired, because the input data are frequently flawed. The efferent doctrine tends to incur very heavy costs in terms of the structures necessary to exercise control and continually to keep in check dissenting voices.

Afferent doctrine

By contrast, the afferent doctrine, which is 'bottom-up' (Figure 8.6), is characterized by a series of individual actions by which the whole is formed like a jigsaw puzzle by a process of aggregation. Decisions tend to be conservative and biased towards the *status quo*, and towards the powerful. The main disadvantage is the difficulty in defining objectives, policing, and/or co-ordinating actions. However, this management style is more likely to be equipped with the true picture of the internal and external environments of the enterprise. General practice is organized on the basis of the afferent doctrine, whereas Trusts are organized along the efferent line. The logic of this dual approach is difficult to fathom.

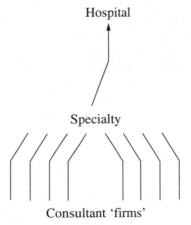

Hospital

Specialty

Consultant 'firms'

Figure 8.6: 'Afferent' doctrine of management.

Which doctrine for the NHS?

The health professions attract a high proportion of staff with a moral rather than materialistic commitment to their work. Small in size and autonomous, the units of service delivery are numerous and diverse. It is not possible, therefore, for 'top-down' management to get an accurate picture of what is going on on the 'shop-floor'. To be efficient in these circumstances, management requires, as a minimum, extensive and minute-by-minute contact (ie feedback) with each unit of the service. This is impractical. Hence, the efferent doctrine of management is not suitable for the NHS. This is amply demonstrated by the fact that every management initiative so far devised for the service has failed, and every decade or so there has been a new one. NHS management has failed time after time after time because it is concentrated on the macro level. What each reorganization has failed to address is the logistics of managing the 'shop-floor' units or firms which actually deliver the service.

The NHS has certain characteristics which make the afferent doctrine of management the most appropriate. Its vast size (over one million employees) imposes the classic dilemma of leadership and control. It is staffed at the point of delivery by highly skilled, highly educated and highly paid professionals, whose power and authority derive from their status, and who are not favourably disposed towards bureaucratic control. There is a tiered system of authority from the Secretary of State to local Trusts, so that it is exceedingly difficult to get functions and control right at each level. It is part of the public sector, which the government is seeking to contract. The product of the NHS is a changed human being (ie cured patient) and, hence, there is intense personal commitment on the part of the professional staff. The inputs, processes and outputs are not standardized as in industry, for patients are of infinite variety and the diagnostic and therapeutic processes, although personal, involve high technology. The NHS subserves several functions simultaneously – provision of health care, teaching and research. The key relationships are few (ie staff, patients and managers) but vitally important, and the stakeholders are many and have differing expectations.

'Custom-made' approach

Thus, the NHS poses special challenges which demand a 'custom-made' approach to management. Hitherto, there has been little academic debate with regard to the NHS *vis à vis* its organization and management theories. Since 1948, change has come about only as a result of political imperatives. Without much debate or much input from the 'shop-floor', the service has moved from a system of planned health care to one in which decision-making is chaotic and in response to an artificially created 'market'. The new situation necessitates that the 'frontline workers', especially doctors, take on controlling managerial roles, since they are the key determinants of the effectiveness of the service.

The involvement of clinicians in management is necessary not simply because they are the main source of expenditure, which in any case is irrelevant, but because they are the only means of minimizing 'running costs'. General management invariably results in:

• *overmanning* – the NHS is probably the most overmanned enterprise in the UK today

• *inappropriate priority-setting* – managers have no firsthand knowledge of the 'business'.

A further advantage of management by clinicians is the fact that professional hierarchies have a short span of control, so that decisions can be made relatively quickly as well as acted upon immediately. The 'shop-floor' in the NHS is doctor led (Figure 8.7) and, therefore, the new management initiative should reflect this. Frontline management

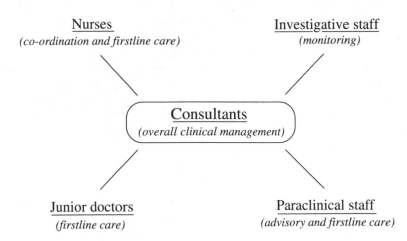

Figure 8.7: The NHS 'shopfloor'.

is the key determinant of the efficiency of the NHS and should be the foundation upon which the NHS management is built.

Comparisons with the university model

The university is the nearest model to the NHS. In the university, management (ie administration) is a separate corps from the faculty (ie academic staff). The faculty has almost total *de facto* governance of the institution. It has a monopoly over the direction and control of 'production' (ie teaching and research). The tasks of administration are mostly the provision and maintenance of the infrastructure, the logistic support of the primary function of the university and the clerical operations of record-keeping, accounting, etc. There are three parts to the work of the academic – teaching, research and 'management'. 'Management' includes those matters, which, although distinguishable from teaching, are nevertheless inseparable from it. In addition, each academic is expected to participate in 'policy-making' at departmental, faculty or university-wide levels. A significant number spend a large proportion of their time running departments and faculties as heads and deans.

The chief executive of a university (ie the vice-chancellor) is usually an academic; deans of faculties and heads of departments are 'fund-holding' academics, not managers. Managers and academics are organized in two parallel structures, academic and non-academic, and one does not interfere with the other. Managers do not tell academics what to teach or what to research. The customers (ie students) have the freedom to choose for themselves which universities to go to and which subjects to study. Schoolteachers do not purchase higher education for their pupils. Local education authorities do not determine how higher education is run, organized or paid for. Unlike the consultant, the academic is left in peace to determine his/her own pattern of work.

The university set-up is a testimony to the fact that general management is not necessary for a public service to be successful. Cost-effectiveness means achieving a given output with minimum cost input. The universities have been able to do this by ceding a significant amount of managerial work to academics. To be cost-effective, the management of NHS Trusts has to be organized along the same lines. Two-thirds of NHS income is spent on staff wages. If these costs could be reduced, and they could by a very extensive retrenchment of 'non-frontline' staff, there would be more money available for patient care. The doctor's work is a trichotomy similar to that of the academic and comprises clinical work, research and 'management', for there is an inseparable managerial element in all professional work. Like academics, doctors accept collective responsibility for the provision of a service to the community. This obliges their direct involvement in 'policy-making' at all levels within a Trust.

Of the three functions traditionally ascribed to general management – policy formulation, line activities and staff activities (Figure 8.8), only staff activities are truly managerial. Policy formulation is usually carried out by a board, whereas line activities in the context of the NHS are in the domain of the professionals. Therefore, the task of managing the 'frontline' ought to be delegated to the professionals. Certain aspects of hospital work, such as outpatient departments, operating theatre departments and medical records departments, which are indispensable to clinical work, are notoriously inefficiently run. They should be brought under the direct managerial control of the clinicians who use them (Figure 8.9). Tasks which are not strictly managerial, such as contracting for the 'internal market', should be

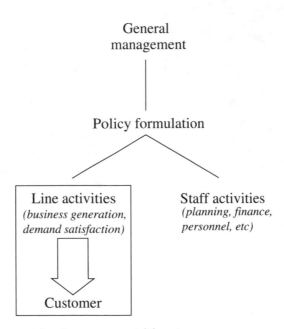

Figure 8.8: Managerial and non-managerial functions.

undertaken by the clinicians who are expected to deliver these contracts. This will allow management to concentrate on what it does best, that is, staff activities such as planning, finance, support and personnel.

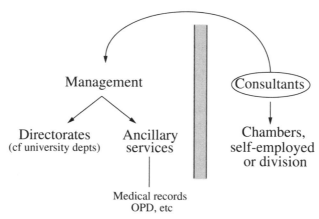

Figure 8.9: Consultants and management.

Epilogue

Apart from religion and the military, human endeavour was previously organized and managed along family lines. In spite of this, enduring and magnificent edifices such as temples and pyramids were erected. As population increased, however, people faced increasing hardship (ie there was economic depression), and as a consequence, began to offer their labour for a wage. This led to the development of the industrial society and with its appearance, enterprise became separated from the family but, crucially, the family retained control by installing managers as a form of 'capital'.

As people have become affluent, however, skills have supplanted brawn as the main economic resource of man – this is why today's politicians stress training as important to economic renewal. However, the mechanism for organizing the work-place has stood still, frozen in the 1930s. It is no surprise, therefore, that the rise of management has failed to fulfil the promise of permanently increasing prosperity. Economic depression has yet again become the norm and naturally people are again looking for an answer. The intractable and global nature of the present 'economic crisis' suggests that management has outlived its usefulness as the engine of the economy. The age of management is over; economic power no longer depends simply upon the ability to organize. Alternatives need to be found; perhaps the focus needs to be shifted towards the wealth creators (ie the professionals).

Dissatisfaction with the new NHS management is not caused solely by a clash of cultures between managers and professionals, but also by inherent contradictions in management practices. Hence, the problems are universal and are observed in other organizations, such as British Rail, the Post Office and British car companies. Firstly, managers are not good at managing people. There is nothing in their training that equips them for this function. Secondly, there are serious flaws in organizational structures. The focus of managers and of management theories is the organization – how to maximize efficiency, how to increase profit, how to manipulate factors internal to the organization, such as span of control, authority and relationships – and they use this to inform job and work designs.

By contrast, the focus of workers, including health professionals, is the product, the service being immediately provided – how to improve the environment of work, how to improve quality, how to improve one's expertise and how to use this to inform job and work designs. With such a dichotomy of views, conflict is inevitable. This manifests itself as industrial problems, which bedevilled British industries in the 1960s and 1970s. It is responsible for the apparent resistance of workers to so-called change. Management deals with this conflict by restrictive practices because of their very negative view of workers, whom they regard as 'the problem'. Most managerial decisions are made, consciously or unconsciously, in the light of this view.

All management involves hierarchy, but the manager's view of it differs from the worker's. In *managerial bureaucracies*, it is not necessary to understand the business of an organization in order to run it. You become leader and exercise authority not because of any personal attributes but because of your position in the hierarchy. Therefore, in the new NHS, managers were recruited from outside. There is nothing more demotivating than this. Workers tend to view hierarchy within the confines of their own trade or profession; in terms of experience and expertise (ie *professional hierarchies*). It is by these measures that all of us climb up the professional ladder. Hence, this type of hierarchy is motivating.

With *bureaucratic hierarchy*, it is inevitable that there will be a strained relationship between managers and workers. This usually manifests as dissent and/or disloyalty. How does management deal with this structural inadequacy? – by techniques designed solely to emasculate dissenting groups. As a result of the differing views of hierarchy, workers have a very negative view of managers, whom they perceive as the sole beneficiaries of the organization; and totally lacking an understanding of the ethics and the environment of work. Managers frequently reinforce this perception by the way they arbitrarily change working practices and conditions of service. The *bureaucratic model* is totally unsuitable for the NHS with its unpredictable work-load, work autonomy and one-to-one provision. NHS management needs to be redefined.

When a group of people are brought together, it is inevitable that there will be chaos and friction between individuals and groups. Chaos requires organization and friction requires lubrication. People are best organized on the basis of belonging, for example, as members of a clinical 'firm' or 'work gang'. Leadership is self-selecting and the environment created is motivating. Relations between groups can be established on the basis of negotiation and amity can be maintained by communication and adequate flow of information. Organization implies tasks to be performed and places to perform these tasks. Tasks are most amicably shared and organized on the basis of consultation between workers, not by edict, as advised by management theorists. The ideal work environment is that which is determined and designed by those who will work in it.

Index

Note: page references in *italics* indicate figures; there may also be textual references on these pages